CONFESSIONS OF A KEY WEST CABBY

Michael Suib
edited by Nancy Butler-Ross
Illustrations by Joe Forte

SeaStory Press
305 Whitehead Street, Suite 1
Key West, FL 33040
www.seastorypress.com

Library of Congress Cataloging-In-Publication Data
Suib, Michael: Confessions of a Key West Cabby
Key West
Miami Herald columnist
Butler-Ross, Nancy
Forte, Joseph
ISBN: 0-9673704-4-2
Cover Art: "Durty Harry's" © by Joe Forte, 2003
Interior Art by Joe Forte, 2003
Book design, cover design by Sheri Lohr, SeaStory Press

CONFESSIONS
OF A KEY WEST
CABBY

MICHAEL SUIB

EDITED BY NANCY BUTLER-ROSS
ILLUSTRATIONS BY JOE FORTE

2003
SeaStory Press
Key West, Florida

"This is dedicated to the one I love."

OTHER BOOKS BY MICHAEL SUIB:

Meditation Express: Stress Relief in 60 Seconds Flat

[with Nancy L. Butler-Ross]

Contents

Cabby Wisdom   19

We're Not In Kansas Anymore   55

The River of Duval   97

Love   129

Southernmost Homeless   165

About the Author, Editor, and Illustrator   198

ILLUSTRATIONS BY JOE FORTE
COVER ILLUSTRATION:

Rick's-Durty Harry's-Tree Bar Entertainment Complex

208 Duval Street, is a Key West Landmark, and is considered by many to be the entertainment "Center of The Universe." Owner Mark Rossi's Midas touch has earned Rick's the reputation as the place to see, and be seen, when in Key West. At night, the taxi stand in front of Rick's is filled with pepto-pink cabs.

Blue Heaven   18

729 Thomas Street, is located in Bahama Village, an oasis of authentic Key West. This restaurant is a charming reminder of the days when Ernest Hemingway refereed boxing matches in the backyard. As then, roosters now still pursue chickens around your feet, with unending tropical gusto. Prominent in the outside eating area is a huge Spanish lime tree, its rope swing surrounded by works of local artisans and the aromas of an eclectic, delectable menu.

The Green Parrot Bar   54

601 Whitehead Street, is the first and last bar on U.S. Route 1 and has been voted one of "The 10 Best Bars in America." It is a Key West landmark watering hole, known for its friendly, funky atmosphere and its official motto of "No Sniveling," since 1890. Its weathered wood bar sits underneath a giant parachute that is witness to poetry slams, fiddling and tattoo contests, and other assorted feats of mayhem.

Angelina's Pizza   96

208 Duval Street, is an institution in its own right. It is located in the Rick's-Dirty Harry Alleyway and is famous world-wide for its pizza specials and reasonable prices. Key West cab drivers who use a code system for placement refer to the downtown code as "pizza," when cruising lower Duval Street, thanks to Angelina's.

Curry Mansion Inn & Museum   128

511 Caroline Street, is a wonderful Victorian mansion, and was the home of Florida's first millionaire, William. F. Curry. This beautifully maintained inn is filled to the brim with antiques, and is a romantic gem, managed to perfection by Edith Amsterdam and her very adept entourage. To visit this lovely house is like stumbling into an 18th Century wonderland, and the view from its widow's walk is spectacular.

Bone Island Bob's   164

430 Greene Street, sits just off the intersection of Greene and Duval Streets. It is chock-full of Key West goodies. Bob's sign, which reads *Beer, Butts & Booty*, only tells half of the story. From the several barstools that sit on the wooden porch facing the street, you can enjoy the parade of characters who stroll by, a gourmet coffee, or a beer at a price that won't break you.

ACKNOWLEDGEMENTS

If anyone had told me, three and one-half years ago, that I would, one day be writing a weekly column for *The Miami Herald*, and publishing a book of those columns, I would have told them, in my most profound and dignified New York accent, "Faggedabowdit."

But write them I did, but not without a little help from my friends, which includes, but is not limited to, the following:

Nancy Butler-Ross, friend, partner, wife, and soul mate, and my personal editor-in-chief who helps to mold my scribblings into a more readable compote, digestible by someone other than myself.

Mark Howell, who as my editor at *The Key West Citizen* trusted the poet in me, and for over two years allowed me to write my columns, and gladly made room for an occasional poetic waxing of mine to appear as well. Thanks also to his wife, Jan, for being a strong ally of my writing.

Michael Haskins, my colleague at *The Key West Citizen*, for his support and kind words.

Jay Ducassi, my editor at *The Miami Herald*, who saw something that he liked, that did not quite fit into the cookie cutter mold of most major newspapers, but said, "Yes," anyway. His continued encouragement and advice, are, to me, priceless commodities.

The Miami Herald's staff, who have patiently contended with my novice's questions, and answered them with equal patience.

To Dave Barry for allowing me to share his kind words, which appear on the back cover of this book.

Eternal gratitude to Herbert and Judith Suib, who

introduced Nancy and me, and for their continued support.

There is a near endless list of kudos to offer to my live-a-board friends at the Garrison Bight Marina in Key West, and my many friends through-out the Keys who wave and greet me when I pass.

The wonderful crew of taxi drivers who work in the City of Key West, and the people on the streets, who never fail to stop and give me either a piece of their mind, or a pat on the back.

I would also like to thank the authors of the hundreds of emails that I have received from around the world in response to my column, and my very humble thanks to those of you who read my column either from the newsstand or the Internet.

Finally, a special thank you, to Joe Forte, the universal artist and poet whose fine artwork graces this book, and to Sheri Lohr, our Publisher at SeaStory Press, who made sure it all worked.

To all of you a heartfelt thank you, thank you, thank you.

Michael Suib

INTRODUCTION

It is 10 a.m. on New Year's Day 1992. The sun is shining brightly in Woodstock, New York where I live, surrounded by the beauty of an evergreen forest and a blistering white landscape of 18 inches of freshly fallen snow. It is breath-taking scenery, which causes me to pause in appreciation, but the wind chill factor this day is minus 20 degrees, with the thermometer hovering around the zero degree mark. A stiff northeast wind is coming in parallel to my sinus cavity, and survival is about all that I can think about.

I am on an emergency mission, and am bundled up appropriately in several layers of arctic wear, stocking cap, muffler, gloves and silk socks. I am armed with a hammer and a chisel, and as I climb the ladder that will deposit me atop my roof, I seriously question my sanity.

The previous night's storm had caused an ice jam to form on the edge of my roof which, as it melted under the bright sunshine, was dripping rapidly into my home office directly below. I plop my self down on the roof, and gird myself for the ordeal of carefully chipping away the frozen concoction without punching holes in my relatively new roof. It is slow work and half an hour later the job is done. My gloves, soaked through to half frozen fingers, are now discarded, and the wind howls a last challenge at me as I rise to start my descent. But I find that the combination of sunshine and my own body heat has frozen the seat of my pants rock solid to the roof of my house.

A Peter, Paul and Mary song echoes through the frozen caverns of my mind and ultimately contributes to the fateful decision that is to change my life. Humming the tune to "Leaving on a Jet Plane," I carefully remove my boots. I slide myself out of my frozen Levi's and then, putting my boots back on, sans pants, I climb back down the ladder.

As I re-enter the house, my cheeks, nose and other wind-burned, red appendages scream for revenge. My then fiancé, now wife and editor-in-chief, Nancy, looks at me standing in the doorway with my boots on but missing my pants, and advises me that she has just deleted, and cannot recover, three months of data entry work on her new computer. Cumulatively, we are not amused, and I say three little words, "Travel Agent, NOW!"

The following day the travel agent delivers as promised, and sends us as far south as possible within the confines of the continental United States: Key West, Florida. Ahhh!

After two weeks of glorious sunshine and gentle breezes, without any wind chills attached, I have made up my mind that somehow, someway, I am going to shed my snow shovel and live in this southernmost city paradise, "even if I have to drive a pink cab to do it." Nancy, never having been fond of the northern frozen tundra, concurs.

A decade, and then some, has passed, and the words "snow shovel" are no longer a part of my vocabulary. I am now living the life in Paradise that most people tell me is their dream. Perhaps it is, but Paradise has a price. Steamy, hot, almost endless summers, in a low paying, two job kind of town, where if you're not employed within the tourist industry, you are what they call, in layman's terms, "unemployed."

To make ends meet in Key West one wears many

hats. I have worked on a "line crew" for a cruise ship, and run a home and business inventory service. Nancy and I have written a book entitled *Meditation Express: Stress Relief In 60 Seconds Flat*, which has been a Book of the Month Club selection. We have also done stress reduction seminars. For the past several years I wrote "Confessions of a Key West Cabby" for *The Key West Citizen*. I now pen "Taxi in Paradise," which appears each Sunday in *The Miami Herald*. And, yes, I still do drive a pink taxi In Key West.

This book is a compilation of Nancy's and my favorite stories: vignettes of life and laughter, pathos and humanity, as seen through the panoramic window of my Pepto-pink cab. These are different from the usual articles that you might expect to read in a daily newspaper. They are poetic glimpses and observations that find the absurd in the mundane.

No meter will be running, so come on along for the ride. I think that you will enjoy it.

Blue Heaven
729 Thomas Street

I

Cabby Wisdom

My job description makes me equal parts driver, therapist, pastor, poet, consultant, and sage. Add to that a liberal sprinkling of baby sitter, comedian, delivery person, and pet watcher. Top with a generous serving of tour guide and a dollop of Miami Herald columnist, and you've just about got it all.

I have given advice to honeymooners and divorcees. I have listened to problems, protestations, and propositions from a dichotomy of individuals, ranging from hard-luck stories from people without two dimes in their pockets, to hard luck stories from millionaires. I have many times been tempted to borrow, from Robert DeNiro's taxi driver character, Travis Bickle, the famous line,
"You talkin' to me?"

WHAT DOES A CABBY KNOW?

The sky darkened. A gossamer veil covered the bright sun as the blue sky and its white pop-corn-puff clouds were overtaken by an ominous gray sheet of thunderheads galloping in over the Atlantic Ocean. Chickens bobbed their heads, propelling themselves to a secure roost, and pelicans, gray and almost invisible against the encroaching storm, flapped their way to safety. Before the first rumble of thunder was heard by human ears, a cacophony of barking dogs heralded its arrival.

The four passengers in my taxi were decked out in a bright array of beach clothing, and looked at the sky with little concern. Mac, the spokesperson for the group, said definitively to no one in particular, "The Weather Channel said sunny and clear. It's not going to rain." The rest of the group nodded.

"Probably just wind clouds," was Mac's next contribution. And again the rest of the group shook their heads in agreement.

No one had asked for my opinion, and experience had taught me to keep my advice to myself, especially when my opinion might be bad news, and could lead to something akin to killing the messenger.

The two women were busily slathering on suntan lotion. Mac and his buddy Charles were already three jumps ahead, and planning where and when to go for dinner, when the distant sound of thunder rolling across the sea caught everyone's attention. The cab was quiet for a moment, the group holding its collective breath waiting to see, or hear, if the noise would repeat itself. Shafts of sunshine piercing the clouds gave hope that the storm would pass. Perhaps.

Silence prevailed as we pulled up to the beach. But the approaching darkness on the horizon had instigated an exodus, as seabirds scurried low along the shoreline seeking sanctuary, and dozens of beach-goers began to gather their clothing, towels, volleyballs, and children, in expectation of heavy weather. Still, there was no request for my cabby wisdom.

As the group prepared to exit my cab, they opened the doors and found that we were surrounded by a throng of people all hoping to get into my little pink taxi, all of them looking to "get outta Dodge" before the deluge.

Thus started the great debate. The women looked at the sky and the large number of people set to flee the beach, and were having more than just second thoughts about their sunny day. They finally asked for my opinion, which I now felt safe to give. Short and to the point, I went for the jugular. "It's going to rain like hell."

The ladies were resolute, and were waving potential passengers away from the taxi's doors. "We're going back to the hotel, it's going to pour, even the cabby says so!"

Mac, now only the official spokesperson for Charles, dug in and responded, somewhat unkindly, "What does the cabby know? The Weather Channel said it would be a sunny day."

"You two stay if you want to, but we're leaving," said Charles' wife.

The lines, then, were drawn. It was the women and myself against the men. I liked the odds. Mac and Charles leaned down and looked into the taxi at me, but I was still stinging from Mac's "What does the cabby know?" remark, so all I could do was shake my head and repeat, "It's going to rain like hell."

I made an illegal U-turn, leaving the men curbside, and we headed back to the women's hotel, sans spouses. The ladies were laughing, and Sue, Mac's wife, added to their good time by saying, "I hope you're right and they get soaked, or else we'll never hear the end of it."

As I started to support my rain theory, day turned to night, and in several heartbeats the light breeze accelerated from an angel's breath to Poseidon's fury, and great gusts of wind swept up leaves and debris. The first drop fell. It plopped and splattered a cupfull of rain against my windshield. The drop, singularly enormous, was followed by another, and then another, as rain began to fall in torrents. The women were gleeful, laughing and clapping with the joy of it all. Driving past rows of conch houses, we saw the rain beating a Samba line across their tin roofs, and heard thunder punctuate the staccato rhythm announcing the Rain God's wrath.

I asked the ladies if they wanted me to turn around and gather up the men. They only laughed harder. I took that as a "no."

The husbands would not be happy that night.

THE THREE STOOGES

Agroup of three men, well dressed by Key West standards, but slightly ajar, flagged me as I was just passing Sloppy Joe's on Lower Duval Street. They had had a few and were in high spirits and at first glance, they appeared to be feeling no pain.

After the usual preliminaries such as, "How's it goin'?, enjoying your stay?, where are you folks from?, where can I drop you?," and the expected responses, "It's going great, this place is a blast," and, "we're from Des Moines," the leader of the pack slipped in, "So where's the hookers?"

This was actually the first time anyone had asked me that question, and for a quick minute I wasn't quite sure how to answer. Sure the question ticked me off. Had I gotten so seedy looking since moving to Key West full-time a year ago that I had 'pimp' written on my forehead? But hey, three drunks from Iowa, how ticked can you get?

So I took the path of least resistance and tried to humor the three musketeers. But I had underestimated the percent of alcohol that these fine gents had floating around in their blood systems, and found myself with three ill-humored, Midwestern drunks in the back seat of my pepto pink cab, determined to find themselves "a good time." It had become my "job" as Hank, the leader of this band bluntly put it, to find them something "different."

After driving around for a couple of minutes and realizing that two out of three of my passengers were nodding off in the back seat, and Hank was off somewhere in an alcohol induced Nirvana, I zeroed in on the destination of my choice and brightly announced, "Here we are guys, that'll be $4.50 please, be careful when you get out and just go through those doors and you'll be in for a treat."

Hank threw some bills at me, poked and pushed his gruesome two-some out the door of the cab, and I drove away leaving the bewildered crew, heads swiveling and bobbing, standing in front of *Ripley's Believe It or Not Odditorium.* Not quite what they were looking for, but they had asked for something different!

Funny thing, though, as I drove back up towards Sloppy Joe's for my next excursion over the rainbow, I realized, with some degree of satisfaction, that I didn't have the faintest idea where one could find a hooker in Key West.

IT TAKES A REAL MAN TO DRIVE A PINK CAB

Eight cabs, and of course their drivers, were sitting at the airport waiting for the next wave of tourists to fly into Cayo Hueso for a few days of sun and surf. Well, okay, scratch the surf part.

A passenger car sat at the curb in front of the airport, with a slightly built Spanish gentleman behind the wheel, who appeared to be waiting with his wife and small child, for someone to exit the terminal.

A beat-up van, driven by a lady of considerable proportions, (she outweighed the man by at least a hundred pounds), pulled up next to the gentleman. The large woman jumped out and started to shout and holler and flail her hands at the very much-surprised man. She was extremely agitated as she shook her fist inches from his face.

The man said nothing.

She accused him of cutting her off on South Roosevelt Boulevard, just outside of the airport. She was running back and forth, from the man to her front bumper, pointing and shouting all the while about what a stupid little S.O.B. the man was. The woman was attracting quite a crowd with her violent display, including one of the officers from the Sheriff's Department who is stationed at the airport.

The officer approached the woman, listened to her

for a moment, and then asked her to please stop shaking her fists and cursing at the man. Actually, he had to ask her twice because she ignored his first request, but finally she did quiet down.

Still the gentleman said nothing.

By this time it had become apparent that one of the reasons the man had not responded was that he spoke little or no English. This only served to agitate the burly woman once again, as she proceeded to curse at the man and scare the daylights out of his family.

The Sheriff was able to sort things out after determining that there was, indeed, no visible damage to either vehicle, and he advised everyone that the matter was closed.

Before getting back into her van though, the woman, shouting one last obscenity, added, "And why don't you go back where you came from!"

It was the type of intolerant, ignorant, phobic insult that you hoped not to hear in Key West. But there it was nonetheless, and though the man and his family spoke little English, it was obvious from the hurt look on their faces that they had understood that last epitaph.

"Shame on you," a strong voice burst forth from our group of cab drivers. "Shame on you!"

Perhaps the woman was indeed ashamed, for without another word, she got into her van and drove away.

Those three words, spoken in defense of strangers, came from the heart, from the essence of what makes Key West a special place.

It also came from the only woman cab driver out of our group of eight.

So, who was it who said, "It takes a real man to drive a pink cab?"

TEENY WEENY BIKINI

The young woman was standing near Smather's beach between two of the mobile concession stands on South Roosevelt Boulevard. She was long and slender and had hair that was the color of spun gold, and as the sun touched her head a luminous cloud seemed to surround her. She was an angelic vision.

I stopped my taxi near the curb and she bounced into the back seat and slammed the door behind her. My windows rattled, as did I, as she spilled a solid stream of primary expletives (*&%^$@#!&*%) into the cab, while thumping vigorously on the back of my car seat. *So much for angelic*, I thought.

Not knowing where my fare wanted to go, we were still sitting at the curb as she ran out of steam and four-letter words. She was wearing a particularly skimpy bathing suit, and was fresh off the beach, so I was fairly certain she wasn't carrying a concealed weapon, and bravely I ventured, "So, how's it goin'?"

"How's it *goin'*?" This was mimicked back to me in disbelief.

"I'm on my honeymoon with an idiot, that's how it's goin'."

The woman, her eyes filling with tears, told me her tale of woe. She and her new spouse had dated nearly five years and almost never fought about anything. Now, three days into their honeymoon, they were fighting about everything.

With a quivering voice, the woman, Brenda, said her new husband did not approve of her bathing suit, and that they had been arguing about it all morning. He had told her that now that they were married she should act more conservatively.

"This coming from a man with a tattoo of a spider on his cheek," she shared.

Her arms, that had been crossed, now opened as she asked me if I thought that her bikini was "too much."

It was a good thing that she had phrased her question as she did. Instead of focusing on the postage-stamp size of her outfit, I was able to truthfully respond, "No, it certainly is not too much."

She was starting to get worked up again, so I interrupted and asked her, "Where to?"

"Maybe back to Chicago," she answered, as tears started to flow.

I saw this as a job for Super Cabby Therapist, and I changed into my analyst's hat; faster than a speeding manic-depressive, able to leap tall phobias in a single bound.

I started with, "Tell me about him."

She took a deep breath and began, "He's handsome and kind, but this is starting to bug me."

"Uh-huh," I answered.

"He always treats me with respect, just like he treats his mother," was her next piece of the puzzle.

"Hmmm...," *very Freudian*, I thought.

"I can't figure this possessive thing out; it's very strange."

"I see," was my next analytical observation.

"What, what do you see?" Brenda asked me.

"What do *you* see, Brenda? That's what is important." This is just more psychobabble that I present, but Brenda grasps at it like a drowning person does a life preserver.

"Oh, I get it. He loves me!" She exclaimed this with

a mixture of joy and confusion, just as there was a knock on my cab's passenger window.

"C'mon, Brenda. I'm sorry." This was said by a somewhat overweight man with dark wavy hair and a tattoo of an arachnid on his cheek. Handsome, though, as Brenda had said.

He was barefoot, and had two beach towels haphazardly draped around his shoulders. He was wearing the smallest men's thong bathing suit that I had seen in quite a while (and I have seen quite a few). He was holding out a long terry cloth beach robe in the hope that his wife would slip into it. He was shaking it at her. "Will ya' cover up already? Let's go back to the beach and talk about it, huh?" Then he stood by quietly, robe dangling, and waited for her answer.

I ventured a wild guess, "Your husband?"

Taking a deep breath and nodding her affirmation, she exited my taxi, and entered the robe that her husband was now wrapping around her. *The cab's meter was still silent.*

It was my turn to sigh, as I put my cabby hat back on and thought that Brenda was right the first time. *She is on her honeymoon with an idiot.*

BEEN THERE, DONE THAT

Iwas driving two out-of-town business-type gents
to the airport last week, and in between cell
phone calls they talked about a competitor of theirs they
were having some difficulties with.

"Now's the time to start litigation," said businessman #1. "He's undercapitalized and doesn't have the
money to defend a lawsuit."

But businessman #2 argued, "Not much of a lawsuit to hang our hat on here."

"Not the point," said businessman #1, waving his
cell phone like a baton. "Hit him hard and kick him while
he's down. Worst that happens is the suit is dropped and
he'll have to dig deep to pay his lawyers. Sounds like a
win-win situation to me."

After depositing these two fine guys at the
American Eagle end of Key West's vast terminal, I headed
back to town and thought about my last fare. Shaking
my head at their analytic and cold-hearted approach
towards a competitor's plight, I stopped myself with a
realization.

My goodness, I thought, *I used to be one of those
guys, cell phone and all.*

Hopefully not as cold-hearted, but no doubt about
it, I in my former life, was a "suit." Business and the
acquisition of more business was my prime motivator,
and I worked hard at it for 14 hours minimum each day,

seven days a week. The importance of each of my decisions directly affected the bottom line of my firm's balance sheet.

To steal a line from an old TV commercial, "I've come a long way, baby."

My life no longer revolves around a "bottom line." An important decision for me these days is whether or not I should use Catherine Street or United Street to get back downtown. Uncomplicated.

I meet people: tourists who fall in love with our weather, our friendliness and our laid back attitudes, and locals who always comment on low pay, high rent, street construction and the other irritants of life here—and then continue on about their great friends, the fantastic weather and what a great sail they had on Tuesday.

Key West is a mixed bag of pluses and minuses, but the thing that sets us apart from most other places is not so much that Key West is in the sunny state of Florida but that Key West is a sunny state of mind.

A wonderful man, also a "suit" but with a disposition fitting our island, left me a lingering thought that same day. He'd finished a five-day, combination business and pleasure trip here, and told me that whenever he comes to Key West, he feels as if he is a mere minute from his soul.

I know the feeling. Ahhh, life is good!

AN INFORMED ELECTORATE?

Election Day, 2000. On this date we are all allowed the privilege of choosing the person to lead us into the new millennium. To many, this is a sacred trust, to others, a popularity contest. The politicos take credit for everything. They did it first, they did it best, while their opponent did little if anything, and what he or she did, was of course, wrong.

Newspapers, radio, television, the Internet and the U.S. Mail all supply us with enough propaganda via paid advertising to help us make that choice. Our political process invests hundreds of millions of dollars in spreading the word; making sure that everyone is armed with the necessary information to make the right choice. Something about creating an informed electorate?

Driving a cab in Key West, I get to meet people from all around the country and casual conversation does, at times, tread into political waters. I would like to share four quick tidbits heard before Election Day that you might find interesting. These statements, and or questions, do not reflect the understanding of the majority of people that I spoke with, but, well, see for yourself:

1. I don't care who runs for President, I will not vote for Bill Clinton again.

2. The country is not ready for a Jewish President.

3. I'm so happy that George Bush decided to run for President again.

4. Why is Hillary Clinton only running for President in New York?

While the above examples are at the inner sanctum of misinformation, I, wearing my cynic's hat, would volunteer that no matter who wins or loses, we might very well get just what we deserve. So much for an informed electorate.

END NOTE: I wrote this article on Election Day 2000, never dreaming that real life would hand us all a much better story than my forage into American politics. And as you read this, the plot so to speak, thickens. Who would have thought that the Gore-Bush Show could bring us such entertainment?

[Editor's Note: In case you missed it, George W. Bush won.]

THE CABBY'S BIRDING BOOK OF THE KEYS

The Snowbirds, (*Northamericus Fleetus*) are back. What started as an isolated sighting several weeks ago (here a bird, there a bird) has escalated to flocks of pale-skinned heliotropes searching for their place in the sun. The Great Northern Snowbird has several distinct sub-genera though, all of them recently making their way south in a sometimes slow but always steady stream. *The Cabby's Birding Book Of The Keys* describes the various family wings of Snowbird as follows:

Northamericus motorhomus: A large and rather diverse section of the breed, these birds travel south each year and bring their nest along with them. The bus-shaped nests barely manage to transverse our narrow streets, and are of a magnitude that leaves Greyhound feeling nothing short of bus-lust.

Northamericus secondhomus: Also a large branch of the Snowbird family. This group is the owner of multiple permanent nests, one being here in Key West, and a second (and sometimes third) roosting place most often in an area where winters leave the landscape in tundra-like desolation. They usually travel light, and flights of them can be seen almost daily in and around the Key West International Airport.

Northamericus seasonalworkus: This Snowbird has

absolutely no tolerance for cold weather and makes the yearly exodus from all points north to our southern clime, and in the summer retraces that same route north. They can be seen sharing nesting habitats around Key West and several of the nearby Keys. (Note: there have been no sightings ever recorded of a nest at affluent Sunset Key.) They have been known to sometimes alternate sleeping and working schedules so that the nest can accommodate several family units simultaneously.

Lesser and *Greater Northamericus homelessus*: These two variations of the genus are very similar in appearance and at times indistinguishable. Some of these Snowbirds are able to find nesting space for themselves in cars or vans, or sometimes on a friend's back porch. Many are able to fend for themselves and their ever-present puppy-on-a-string by doing odd jobs, or playing melodies on street corners. Most are down on their luck. Others sport signs announcing, *We're ugly, broke and nobody wants us*, or, *Why lie, I need $ for a beer*. Many are not able to do much else other than find a doorway to huddle in. Some, at the largess of the Key West Police Department, find nesting accommodations at the Stock Island Hilton, (aka the County Jail).

While the Snowbirds have returned, we still await the elusive Tourist Bird (*Cashius for-us*) that is still in scant evidence. There have been a few advance specimens roosting and leaving deposits, then taking off for other locales.

In the meantime we Key Westers who depend on tourism for our daily crumbs keep an eye on The Weather Channel, and await the first blast of Arctic air to come barreling out of Canada. Our mantra is, *When it snows, they will come, when it snows, they will come.*

TIPS AHOY!

Jocko (his real name) flagged my cab one after-noon on Caroline Street, out in front of West Marine, and asked me to drive him to the Oceanside Marina on Stock Island. He was a likeable guy wearing an eclectic mix of clothing that drew a smile from me as we wove our way through Old Town detours and North Roosevelt Boulevard traffic. He had on a tattered, but bright, purple and green, tie-dyed tee shirt, a red and white Samurai headband, and white, grease-coated pedal-pusher type pants. On his feet he boasted one neon-green sneaker and one DayGlo orange sneaker (left foot green, remaining foot orange). He was a colorful person indeed. Adding to his image were jet-black hair and a matching mustache.

Jocko told me he was just cruising through, when he encountered some engine trouble on his boat. He'd been in Key West drumming up the parts to do the repairs, and was now headed back to tackle the job.

When we arrived at the marina, I sensed that Jocko's finances might be a bit strained, so I offered him a small "local's discount" that he graciously accepted. He then proceeded to tip me more than generously. Pointing to his boat, a shiny, sixty-plus foot Hatteras Fisherman, he waved good-bye and said,"What goes around, comes around."

Key West is a tourist industry town. In the most

general of terms, if you live in Key West and do not work in a tourist related industry, you are either retired, extremely wealthy, or... what is that word I'm groping for... oh yes, unemployed.

Being a cab driver, where tips comprise an important part of my income, I have met many people, rich and not so rich, who have tipped generously, and for that I am grateful.

May I offer the following Tips for the Tipping Impaired:

1. Tipping is nice. Not mandatory, but nice.

2. A tip is for good service, not poor service.

3. If you're really short on $$$, a thank you is appreciated and understood. (We've all been there.)

4. Reminder: many service workers are paid near-minimum wage, or below, and tips are a matter of survival for them.

Telling the wait-staff or bell person or cab driver about the four hundred thousand dollar building lot that you have just purchased, and then leaving loose change as a tip, is in bad taste, a no-no, and should be reason, in more than just a biblical sense, for your expulsion from Paradise.

These are vague parameters, and good judgment is still the best rule of thumb. Keep in mind that while you're on vacation, having to serve your own food, wash your own dishes, make your own bed, clean your bathroom, carry your own bags and drive yourself to and from the airport or nightspots might not make for much of a holiday.

And now I would like to "tip" my hat and convey my thanks to the many people of Key West's service industry who are by far the best tippers on the island. They are the ones, who like Jocko, understand that what goes around, really does come around.

$12,384.00, GIVE OR TAKE A CAB RIDE OR TWO

It gives your tourists a bad first impression, ya know what I mean? Here they travel a coupla' thousand miles and the first thing they get is an expensive cab ride from the airport." *[Editor's Note: the cab fare, set by the City of Key West, is $7.50 per person.]*

The man giving me his lecture on tourism had just flown in on a private jet from Indianapolis (approximately $4,000), and he and his friend were heading to the Hilton Hotel to spend three nights at one of Sunset Key's beautiful guest cottages ($800 - $1,400 per night).

"There should be a discount rate to get to the hotels, that way you feel like you're more welcome and nobody is trying to take advantage of you. Restaurants are expensive, it's all too expensive, know what I mean?"

I try to keep an open mind when chatting with my various passengers. They do come from all walks of life, and their financial situations are as varied as their personalities. The fact is, everything is expensive in Key West. And it's not just expensive for the tourists who come to enjoy our island paradise, it is expensive for we locals as well. That four-dollar beer costs me about the same four dollars as it does the next guy, whether he is from Marlin Pier in Key West or from Marlin, Texas, and we all know that affordable housing is as elusive as a will-o'-the-wisp. And yes, I even pay the same price for a cab ride when the need arises.

So, I tried to explain to this gent my version of the economics of a sustainable wage, and the importance of allowing the city's service workers to earn enough money to keep themselves afloat (which usually takes at least two jobs to accomplish, in any event). But he was intent on a discount ride to The Hilton, and so was not really interested in my cabby philosophy.

"Hey, I'm paying $500 to go fishing and over $300 to fly to the Tortugas, so all I'm saying is you guys should lower your prices." He then extracts a foot-long cigar and announces, "Cuban," ($65 on the black market), as he sets it between his teeth.

"Sorry sir, this is a non-smoking cab," I announce, as I do to anyone entering with, or trying to light up within the confines of my taxi universe.

Exasperated, the man pulls the cigar from his mouth and sputters, "Ya see what I mean?"

Nope, for the life of me, I cannot!

LITTLE WHITE LIES

Iknow you'll be surprised when I tell you that
driving a cab in Key West is not all glamour and
excitement. There are periods of tedium that encourage
one to be somewhat creative to avoid death by boredom.
So, every once and awhile, I cross my fingers and
unleash an untruth, harmless and without malice of
course, upon one of my passengers.

The recipients of my yarns usually precipitate
them by asking one of several tiresome questions.

"Do you live here?" is an oft-asked question I used
to respond to with blank stares of disbelief. But now it
triggers responses from me as geographically diverse as,
"No, I commute from Miami, Orlando, or Atlanta," or, if
I'm particularly moved, "Chicago." Most passengers get it,
after a beat or two, and I'm rewarded with a shy smile or
embarrassed chuckle.

Another favorite is, "What did you do before you
drove a cab?" Depending on my mood, I have been a
podiatrist, a professor of English at N.Y.U., a stockbro-
ker, a munitions dealer, and an ex-C.I.A. agent, all culmi-
nating in job burn-out.

I recently drove a group up to the Sugarloaf
Airport for a skydiving excursion. The entire group, other
than one very nervous young lady, had previously taken
the plunge at least once, and several had multiple experi-
ences.

Her friends were teasingly supportive, but the woman was having serious second thoughts, and appeared ready to call it off. One of the group asked for my opinion, and I spoke right up, quite sincerely conveying the following:

- It's a piece of cake,
- No problem,
- I've done it dozens of times,
- There's nothing quite like it,
- It's as easy as riding a bike, and
- You'll want to go right back and do it again.

The novice swallowed this hook, line and parachute. With her courage somewhat renewed, she bounded out of the cab, and a short time later, out of a plane, to free-fall from an altitude of 10,000 feet.

When I retrieved the same group later in the day to bring them back into Key West, the woman, a virgin no longer, did in fact, want to go back and do it again. She had had a grand time and fervently thanked me for my words of encouragement.

I then told her the truth, that I had never jumped from a plane, never would, and that the only way you'd get me through the doors of a plane with a parachute on my back was if a football team was to pound me, tie me up, and forcibly eject me. (Okay, color me yellow, but this sport does not appeal to me.)

The perfect ending to this story would be that the young lady forgave me the little white lie, tipped me a handsome sum, and added a hug as a bonus. But, alas, this was not to be. She proceeded to call me the unkindest names before slamming the door of my cab and storming off with her friends.

So, no more little white lies for me.

And if you believe that, perhaps I could interest you in this bridge I have for sale. It's about seven miles long and of recent construction. Low down payment. No reasonable offer refused.

"WHO TOUCHES A HAIR ON YON GRAY HEAD...."

Iwas driving two women to the La-Te-Da Inn this week. In the course of our conversation, one of the ladies told me she thought that I had a great looking mustache, and that my gray hair made me look handsome.

"Tell me more," I said.

"Why is it," she continued, "that when a man with gray hair is called handsome it's a compliment, but when a woman with gray hair is called handsome, she is thought to be over the hill?"

I thought about it for a moment, and had to concede that "handsome" did not quite have the same connotation about a woman as for a man; but "over the hill" might be a bit extreme.

These ladies were both attractive, in fact beautiful, and I told them so.

"We both subscribe to the L'Oreal thesis that we're worth it," said one, "so it's out with the gray and in with the red. We've both been called handsome once too often. Who needs it? Maybe when we're in our seventies it would be nice, but I'm too young to be handsome!"

Farewells said, I left the two attractive women curbside at La-Te-Da, and drove onward to my next stop at La Brisa Condos. There I picked up Mrs. B., a regular, and headed off with her to her appointment with her doctor. Mrs. B. was a nice-looking lady in her early forties, well-dressed with a matching sense of humor. She also had a beautiful head of stylishly cut, gray hair. I mentioned my last passengers' conversation to her, and asked if she would feel it a compliment or not if I told her that she was a handsome woman.

"I'll take it," she said. "In fact, I'll take any compliment that you have to offer."

Semantics aside, many words can mean different things to different people. Is "Reubenesque" chubby or beautiful? Is "husky" muscular or fat? If you're described as having "a great personality," can you still be good looking? And just how attractive, or not, is handsome?

Beauty is within us. Whether we are short, tall, thin or fat, balding or gray-haired, we are only as attractive and young as we feel.

POOF! YOU'RE A PEDESTRIAN

For those who do not know the definition of the term "hat trick," I will explain. It is a hockey term that has come into general usage to describe a successfully completed feat of three accomplishments. Three goals scored in one hockey game is labeled a hat trick. Local fishing terminology has similarly dubbed the landing of a tarpon, a bonefish and a permit on the same outing as a "hat trick." And, I am saddened to say, I had my own personal hat trick while driving my taxi here in Key West. I found bigotry, or rather bigotry found me, not once, not twice, but three times in the same day.

My first encounter was with a well-dressed local man who waved me down on Duval Street at 8:30 a.m. last Monday. He and his companion, a disheveled, semi-coherent gent, who was ripe from a night out on the town, gave me a vague location as their destination. And off I went.

Thirty seconds into this ride, the more dapper of the two asked me, in a severely Teutonic accent, if I was Jewish. Now, this is a somewhat unusual query from a stranger, so I asked him why he would ask a person whom he'd never met a question of such a personal nature.

"Just curious," he slurred. "I've never met a Jewish cab driver before. *Those people* are usually doctors or lawyers."

"Anti-Semite in the aft cabin," I mumbled, shaking my head.

"What did you say?" the dapper man asked.

"I said, I have a magic trick to show you. Want to see it?"

The men were both nodding their heads in hopes of some entertainment when I pulled the cab over to the curb. I hopped out, opened their door and gave them the thumb while pointing to the street. "Poof," I said. "You're a pedestrian."

They walked away a little bewildered, but were cognizant enough to call my parents' marital status into question.

My next excursion with the tolerantly challenged came from yet another Key Wester who, after 30 years here, was moving back north to a little town in rural Michigan that he proudly labeled "the birthplace of the Klan."

"As in Ku Klux?" I asked cautiously.

"Yup, it's a town where a white woman can still walk the streets safely at night."

This Grand Wizard was tossing about derogatory racial epithets at such a rapid pace that I suggested he cool it. He became agitated and abusive. He, too, became a pedestrian with a "poof."

To complete my hat trick, I journeyed to the Key West Airport and picked up two young fellows who had flown in on Cape Air. They were exited about being in town and asked loud questions about places to go and where to hang out.

"You a fag?" one of them suddenly asked.

"Not a bright question," I responded.

"How come?" asked the same man.

Shaking my head in disbelief that within a three-hour time span I'd had the company of three sets of overt bigots, I tried patiently to explain that using that term was not nice, was politically incorrect, offered an extreme display of ignorance, and could, if said to the wrong party, result in hospitalization.

"So, you a fag?" the man asked again.

With a sigh, my response was, "No, I'm a magician... and poof! you're a pedestrian."

It was a discouraging day. The humor in it was if-I-don't-laugh-about-it-I'll-cry.

My last fare of the day was a lady I picked up at a guest-house on Duval Street. As we headed to the airport, she explained to me how, even though she loves Key West, she has had it up to here, indicating the top of her cowboy hatted head.

"It's the riff-raff I can't take, too much riff-raff."

Resigned, I took a deep breath, smiled sweetly and asked, "So, do you want to see a magic trick, lady?"

MAKE MY DAY!

There are certain things that do not mix well within the confines of my cabby universe:

• I do not do well with drunks, which is one of the reasons that I don't drive a cab at night,

• I have no tolerance for bigots who, if after a request to cool it, do not, so I deposit them roadside with the rest of the trash,

• I try not to discuss politics, which is hard.

For some reason people are, at times, determined to make their views mine, and hell hath no fury like a viewpoint scorned.

One of my regular fares is a gentleman of local renown. I have read items in our Key West newspapers by, and about, him. He is outspoken, and has the energy and determination to express his position on many subjects, and so he does. My main problem with him is that he switches positions from conversation to conversation, and isn't happy unless you agree with him.

Each time he rides with me he attempts to get me involved in one or another of his crusades. Little Cuban Elian Gonzales became one of his personal favorites, though he changed sides each week like he was changing socks. He has harassed me through city, county, and now, heaven help me, national elections.

Pro-life, pro-choice, noise ordinances, buses, sewer treatment, open the beaches, close the beaches (life is a beach), death penalties, and late parking ticket penalties are all argued with equal zest.

He has harangued me for not being more involved, yet he attempts to show me the error of my ways when I have gotten involved. I've tried to explain to him that discussing political concerns in five-minute bytes to the back of my head is probably not an optimum position for an exchange of constructive conversation.

But he hears none of this and forges on, trying to inflict his position indelibly upon me before he leaves the cab. I have tried responding in grunts and nods but he has concluded those expressions to be argumentative. I vow not to be drawn into his politics, and sometimes I am successful, and at other-times not so.

This past week I tried a new tact. We exchanged greetings and he told me his destination. He then vented some political scripture in my direction and I ignored him. He pushed on and I ignored him harder. No nods nor grunts. No smiles, frowns, nor any other exclamations or expressions of acknowledgment. I was a rock! His irresistible force had met my immovable object, and I was winning. He huffed and puffed but he could not cleave my resolution. His frustration was obvious, but my calm karma remained intact.

When he left my cab he did so in disgust. He leaned into my window, almost face to face with me. "What kind of intellectual are you? You're nothing but a Pinko, Columnist Cabby."

He had made my day. Someone, after all of these years, has finally called me an intellectual. As for the "pinko" thing... that sounded vaguely familiar.

REAL AMERICAN HEROES

We all do it. We complain about things that, at the time, seem to have great importance. A fender-bender or a car that won't start, a bad hair day or a sore throat. All of us have had our share, and then some, of life's irritants. Awhile back, I was having just one of those days. I got up on the wrong side of the bed, my back ached, and it was downhill from there. I won't bore you with details because you've all been there yourselves.

Midday, I got a call that sent me and my cab to the Washington Street Inn. Waiting in front was a couple from Moscow, Idaho, who wanted to go to the Glassbottom Boat at the foot of Duval Street. Normally an easy trip, this one had a few problems attached. Rick was in a wheelchair, and not able to help at all with his transfer from the chair into the cab. He had broken his back several years before in an accident while playing and wrestling with his teenage son. Now a quadraplegic, his only mobility was from the neck up. He was also diabetic, and he and his wife had lost their daughter to cancer the year before.

Rick and Betty came down to Key West from Orlando, Disney World, Universal Studios and the rest, after attending a National Diabetes Conference where Rick was a featured speaker.

It took about ten minutes to get Rick set up in the

back of the cab. Both he and Betty cautioned me before we started the lifting process, "not to hurt yourself." Rick said with a laugh, "Just drop me if I start falling. You can't hurt me, I won't feel a thing."

With some tugging, belt pulling and sweat, the task was completed and off we went.

One of my claims to fame is that I am The Southernmost Poet, at least the cards with Key West poems that sit on my dashboard announce that fact. Anytime someone in my cab spots one and asks about it, it becomes theirs. Some see them, others do not. I usually have five or six different pieces in view. Rick asked about them. Each in turn was read by either he or Betty. They took the time that no other passengers had before, taking each poem as a new experience. Rick seemed to savor each one, and treated them all with respect. This strong man and his equally strong wife, from Moscow, Idaho took the time to smell the roses. Their grace, charm, good humor and bravery, faced with the hand that they were dealt, left an impression on me not soon forgotten.

I had met a pair of Real American Heroes. No capes or masks or spandex suits, just smiles on their faces, and a determination that this day, each day, would be better than the last.

DENIAL IS NOT A RIVER IN EGYPT

'*Ka-ching*' is the sound of a cash register ringing.

Here it is, the first week in November, Goombay and Fantasy Fest celebrations are successfully tucked under our belts, and we've been surrounded by flocks of Jimmy Buffett's Parrotheads, and flotillas of powerboats. Ka-ching. We have tourists hard at work igniting a dawdling economy with the coin of the realm: the tourist dollar. *Ka-ching*. Hello and Hallelujah, we knew you would be back. It's Key West, how could you stay away?

But into each life, as they say, a little rain must fall. Over the southern horizon looms the specter of Hurricane Michelle, pounding Nicaragua and the coast of Central America, and churning through the Caribbean Sea on a slow meander towards Cuba and then …uh-oh. The tourists begin to get a little nervous as the storm is upgraded to a Category 2 hurricane. They start looking around for solace, and a stroking, as they ask the locals what they think.

"Not a problem."

"She'll turn east."

"She'll turn west."

"Waters are too cool for a bad one."

"It'll break-up once she hits the mountains of Cuba."

A potpourri of information, all meant to calm the

tourists' sense of anticipation (not to mention our own), and keep the local economy lubricated. *Ka-ching.*

As the hurricane intensifies to a Category 3, we locals, experts on matters of hurricanes and cold beer, are again grilled. Parrotheads, whose hats with winged mascots have already blown away in the wind, are now asking more pointedly, "Yeah, but what if...?"

Armed with denial, we locals continue our fearless forecasts:

"Won't even be close."

"Too late in the season for a major storm."

"Key West hasn't had a major hit since 1919."

"Relax and have another beer."

We are, of course, making this all up as we go along because, as usual, we are clueless.

Michelle, now a Category 4 hurricane, is bearing down on us and has become something to pay attention to. The first indication that this could be a serious threat is when Monroe County orders some type of mandatory evacuation. It is a women-and-children-first kind of thing, and for those of us who have seen the movie Titanic...well, lets say it gets my attention.

The power boaters are the first to hit the road with their million dollar toys, followed closely by most of the Parrotheads, and then the locals who have been there, done this before and want no part of the Hurricane party that is brewing. Nor the clean-up afterward.

The wind velocity increases and roads and airlines shut down.

Ka-ching! Supermarkets are selling every battery, potato chip, pretzel and bottle of beer on their shelves. *Ka-ching.* Sheets of plywood and buckets of nails. *Ka-ching.* Boaters' supplies, rail fenders and miles of new line.

Key West got lucky again this time, and the near, or not so near, miss allowed all of us who stayed to exhale a collective sigh of relief. The Key Westers who had journeyed to the mainland were happy that the storm had spared us. The tourists who had left sat in their living rooms in Cleveland or Oshkosh shaking their heads and lamenting about the excitement that they missed.

The boards are now down from the store windows, the airport is back in business, and hotels and guesthouses are busy answering their phones for new reservations. The River of Denial has gotten us safely through another hurricane season. We hope.

Ka-ching!

The Green Parrot Bar
601 Whitehead Street

II

We're Not In Kansas Anymore

The streets of this southernmost city, Key West, Florida, are filled with a never-ending supply of delectably unique and absolutely interesting people, most of whom have percolated their way down U.S. Route 1 to mile marker "0" in search of Paradise.
What they find is not always exactly what they had imagined, but the one thing that most do agree upon is that 'dull' and 'Key West' are not synonymous.
Quirky, the word often used to describe the Southernmost City and its inhabitants is, of course, an understatement. For me, Key West can best be described as being "somewhere over the rainbow."

LIONS AND TIGERS AND BARES

I was in cabby heaven last week. I got the best of two worlds: the nicest flock of Jimmy Buffett 'Parrot Heads' ever to land here were going out to the airport, and Fantasy Fest 1999's "Warptime" revelers were coming back in. The Buffett fans exclaimed, "Wait 'til next year!" and the Halloween 'ghouls' and boys revved up for this year's festivities.

Last year, my first Fantasy Fest as a cabby, was a roller coaster of sights and sightings. Sort of Mardi Gras and the Macy's Thanksgiving Day Parade squeezed into a size-four shoe. I loved it!

One of Key West's best taxi dispatchers begins each of his shifts by announcing, "Okay, boys and girls, take a deep breath, we're off to the circus!" And what a circus it was. Costumes and un-costumes of every hue and shade adorned bodies of every size and shape, some more shapely than others. "Butt"— inhibitions to the wind, the daring dared to grin and bare it. Before the third day of festivities had unfolded, I was suffering from sensory overload.

Never, since the Dutch had traded $28.00 worth of beads for Manhattan Island, have so many beads purchased such an interesting commodity. Driving was a dangerous task, the sights so colorful, that the possibility of whiplash lurked around every corner. The costumes ranged from wonderfully outrageous to outrageously wonderful, and the air held the pungent aroma of party-time.

My last fare of Fantasy Fest eve was a lovely senior citizen couple from the Midwest. Eyes wide with excitement, they sat quietly in the back seat holding hands. An air-brushed, bare-breasted feline had just walked by our cab, orange and black stripes strategically painted on her body. The couple huddled as my tendency toward whiplash kicked into gear. The woman nuzzled her husband and said, "Well dear, I don't think we're in Kansas anymore."

Lions and tigers and "bares"...oh, my!

THOSE PEOPLE!

[Editor's Note: The 'Fat Lady' is drag queen Jim Brown aka Mama Crass, who closes every Fantasy Fest by lip-synching 'God Bless America,' ala Kate Smith. The purpose of Fantasy Fest is to raise funds for an organization called AIDS Help in Key West. For several months prior to October, candidates for King and Queen of Fantasy Fest hold fund-raisers, with the top male and female fund-raisers being crowned as King and Queen.]

By the time this article appears, the 'Fat Lady' has sung, and Fantasy Fest 2000 will be history. You've all had your fill of circuses and clowns, masks, beads, and body paint. 70,000 people, give or take a few thousand, have folded their costumes, packed their greasepaint and their luggage, and before leaving for the airport, have hidden most of their exposed body parts behind some degree of clothing. (Most airlines do have a 'no pants, no flight,' policy.)

Almost without exception, the people I met during Fantasy Fest week were pleasant, conscientious participants in one heck of a party.

Almost!

Two weeks ago, on the day of The Coronation, I picked up a man at the airport who'd come to town for an overnight business trip. He needed, he said, breakfast and directions to City Hall. He had flown down from Miami, and was not particularly happy about spending any quality time in Key West. He was in town, he told me, because of some business he had to take care of with the City and the school board. "I won't be able to get out of town quickly enough," was his response when I asked him if he was going to stay in town for any of the festivities.

I had a feeling that I knew where this conversation was headed, but I played the innocent, and asked the obligatory leading question just the same. "Oh," I asked with the look of a simpleton upon my cheerful face, "why is that?"

"I just think that it's disgusting.   , with their disgusting friends coming down from who knows where. Thousands of them. That's not how it should be!"

Still smiling, I asked the guy if he knew that two of our City Commissioners are gay. Was he still sure he wanted to do business with "those people?"

It took him a few beats to recover his composure. He began to backpedal, making a few urgent attempts to remove his foot from his mouth.

Long story short: I made his trip downtown from the airport as miserable for him as I possibly could. I had a very good time!

This person, I might add, did not tip me when our short period together had expired. Hmmm, I wonder if it was something that I said?

We do live in a city where tolerance is an expected courtesy. "Those people" can be, and usually are, our friends, neighbors, and yes, ourselves. In Key West, being different is the norm, not the exception, and that is why the grandest party of the year here celebrates exactly that uniqueness. Gay or straight, black or white, and everything in between, we are a dichotomy of differences that not so much tolerate each other, as accept each other.

This is a nice place to call home.

MY WIFE IS GONNA KILL ME

"**M**y wife is gonna kill me!" Those were the first words uttered by one slightly intoxicated man who had barely managed to climb into my cab one evening. He and four of his friends were visiting Key West from a town in Georgia, famous for the onions that bear its name proudly, but which will go unnamed to protect the innocent (or not so innocent).

As bits and pieces of the story evolved from this besotted group of Musketeers, it seems that Onionhead numero uno had the urge to splurge, and while out on the town the previous night met a lady of the evening named Pearl. Now Pearl, it seems, was quite a girl, and proceeded to present this gent with a list of options for his carnal pleasure that included, but was not limited to, having himself bound and tethered to a bedpost. Never having encountered this particular morsel before, the man chose very carefully from column number one. But the result was not exactly what he had in mind. He spent the next hour wriggling out of the predicament he'd gotten into.

After untying himself and taking inventory, he found that, along with his humility, his wallet, cash, driver's license, credit cards, pictures of his new wife (yes, a newlywed approaching his sixth month anniversary), his wedding ring was missing.

"Yup, she is gonna kill me for sure," he groaned.

This was one dog-eared puppy, and while I couldn't really feel sorry for him, I did manage to shake my head in consideration of his plight.

His friends were not particularly supportive in his hour of need. He was down, and they were determined to keep him there as they razzed him, each one in turn taking a poke at him (hey, what are friends for), and laughing at his predicament. A few constructive suggestions were tossed about, ranging from contacting the police, which was immediately dismissed, to making the rounds of the local pawnshops, which I personally thought was a pretty good idea.

Onionhead number two asked for my advice and I, tongue in cheek, freely administered it.

"How about the old "Barracuda Ploy?" I offered. "It's very convincing, and your bride will be hugging and pampering you, instead of instituting divorce proceedings. It's a sure winner."

Having the group's undivided attention, I now laid out the plan. "What you do is you chop off your ring finger. Then tell your wife that you went snorkeling, and while exploring the depths off Key West, a Barracuda, thinking your shiny new wedding band was a tasty bit of sushi, took a hefty bite that relieved you of the first two joints of your ring finger, and your wedding band as well."

Instead of eliciting a few laughs, my humble attempt at humor brought, instead, a contemplative silence. These guys were actually considering my suggestion as a possible solution. Thankfully, one of the men whose gray matter was somewhat intact, chimed in with a dismissive, "Nah, it's a little drastic, man. And if she doesn't buy it, he'll be out part of a finger."

The last thing I heard before the group left the cab was something about a car accident and amnesia.

My bet is, his wife is gonna kill him.

DÉJÁ VU

I picked up an attractive middle-aged couple from the Midwest at the airport and they had asked me to drive them to a well-known local resort on Truman Avenue.

"Is it a nice place?" the woman asked. It was a nice place, and that was my response. But the way the conversation was going led me to believe that the woman had no idea the resort we were heading to was "clothing optional." Her partner had said little, and kept a low profile in the back seat while she asked question after question about the resort, its location, the swimming pool, type of clientele, and so on. The question of to-be-clothed or not-to-be-clothed never arose.

As I drove into the resort's parking area, the tell-tale sign hanging from the building's front entrance announced proudly, *Clothing Optional.* This had the effect of stopping the lady, mid-sentence. Her mouth dropped and words ceased to flow. A moment of silence, and then the woman erupted. "Are you crazy? You made reservations at a nudist colony? What were you thinking?"

The man put his hands up in front of himself as a protective maneuver. "Now, take it easy, it's not a nudist colony, it's a clothing optional resort. You can still wear your clothing if you want to." He looked at me for support, but I had none to offer.

"Oh, my God, I can't do this. Why didn't you ask me first, before getting me down here?"

The husband was digging in, sensing that his wife was not wavering in her resolve not to get naked in Paradise.

"Brenda, let's try it. If you don't like it, we'll leave."

After a ten-minute debate, Brenda, her husband and their luggage reluctantly left my cab. The woman wondered out loud why he had bothered to pack clothes if he planned to be naked for five days.

Five days later I was dispatched to a request for my services at the same resort. I remembered the couple, and was surprised they had actually lasted the five days the reservation called for.

"How did it go?" was my first question. Once again the woman was off to the races, but with an unexpected twist.

"It was a blast, I loved it," Brenda shouted as we started off to the airport. "It was the best vacation I ever had." Superlatives flowed like water. Fantastic, invigorating, exciting, were the words that fell into my lap.

Her husband sat still in the back seat. I looked at him through the rear-view mirror. He was frowning and did not appear to be in the best of spirits.

"Don't mind him," said Brenda. "He hated it. He wanted to leave the first day." She relished the turn of events and took every opportunity to rub it in. "I had to practically attack him to get him out of his bathing suit. Can you imagine?"

By the time the couple left the cab, her husband had still not spoken a word. As she said goodbye, she added, "I don't know about him, but it'll be Déjà Vu all over again for me next year."

MURPHY'S LAW

Whatever can go wrong, will go wrong!" We've all heard this edict in one form or another, and most of us have probably been on the receiving end of Murphy's Law. So there maybe a familiar ring to this story.

I'd picked up a group of four people this past week who were impatiently standing in front of the Eaton Lodge on Eaton Street, waving frantically to get my attention. Two attractive, but obviously irate, women got into my cab, along with a pair of teenage daughters.

"We have to go to Stock Island. Our car was towed last night and we have to ransom it, and then be up in Big Pine Key in about half an hour. We're going diving today."

My response of, "I don't think so," brought the conversation to a halt. I explained that both the clock and geography would not get them up to their dive boat in time. I suggested it might be appropriate to put "Plan B" into effect, if they had a Plan B.

Mom #1 said, "We'll see about that," and whipped out her cell phone to call the dive boat to demand that it wait for them. Alas, that was not to be, and when she disconnected her call, she went ballistic with a litany of complaints about all that had gone wrong with their Key West vacation.

The list included the following: the Public Works

Department, the police, the towing company, their travel agent, the innkeepers, the Tourist Development Council, American Airlines, the dive boat, the cab company, and ultimately, moi.

Considering all that had gone awry up to this point, which was only day number two of their vacation, I could understand why they might be a bit upset. But fair is fair.

"What did I do to get on your list? "I asked cheerfully. "I'm only a cabby." Still trying for an upbeat tone to help carry the moment, I added, "You know what they say about Murphy's Law."

The moms were not amused, and Mom #1 gave me a stare that sent chills down my spine despite the tropical weather.

When we arrived at the towing company on Stock Island, the group left the cab, but not before one of the teens clued me in. "Whenever someone mentions Murphy's Law," said the kid, "mom gets bent. Our last name is Murphy."

Murphy's Law strikes again!

A LOST GUESTHOUSE

Amid the congenial madness that is Key West, the human condition displays itself to me each day. Sometimes it is portrayed in the sad, worldly proportions of the homeless, the hungry and the disenfranchised, and at times in comedic vignettes featuring the large number of visitors who trek to Key West each year.

In the lighter vein, I am often enlisted to participate in a quest, which is the cab driver's version of the search for the Holy Grail. Sounds serious! It usually starts off with a passenger's request to find something, someone or someplace, and then is followed by a somewhat fuzzy explanation as to how they lost, misplaced or forgot the whereabouts of said object.

At times the misplaced object is a spouse. "I dropped her off at a clothing store on Duval Street and I was supposed to pick her up in an hour. That was about two and a half hours ago. And all of these stores look alike." So, off we go in search of a store that has tee shirts and shorts in its windows and, we hope, a patiently waiting wife.

Vehicles are another item often lost in Key West. Considering that the circumstances surrounding the loss are usually alcohol related, it's probably a good thing that the drivers misplaced their means of transportation.

"Partied hearty last night and can't remember

where I left my scooter/car/bike, dude," is not an uncommon theme.

Or, "Yeah, a blue Toyota with Iowa plates, somewhere off Duval Street, I think," and off we go on a mission. At times it is an easy find, and other times I have to put out an A.C.B., that is, an All Cabby Bulletin: "Be on the lookout for Iowa plates, #123-XYZ."

That usually does the trick, with one of my fellow cabbies passing the vehicle parked somewhere or another, and calling dispatch with the information. Of course, if that car just happened to have been parked illegally, it might entail a trip to the towing company on Stock Island to bail it out. A journey unto itself.

A short time ago, Tim and his cousin Gary, both from Atlanta, got into my cab about 8:00 AM. Through bloodshot eyes and showing more than just a little wear and tear, they told me their problem. They had arrived in town the previous evening with no lodging reservations and had found a place to stay at a guesthouse. They had deposited their luggage, and their girlfriends as well, and went off to have a couple of beers. Leaving the women to fend for themselves, they drove to Duval Street, where the cousins visited eight or nine drinking establishments. All the rest, they told me, "was a blur."

"Can ya help us, huh?" asked one of the men. "We can't remember the name of the guesthouse we're staying at, or where it's located. And the ladies are going to be very ticked off."

They groaned mightily at that thought. I pumped them for some information that might help to shed some light on our quest, and twenty questions later the best that I could dredge up was that "it had a white picket fence around it."

"Sorry guys," I said. "You're going to have to do a little better than that if we're going to find it."

Other tidbits they remembered about the place were the following: it had a porch, wooden shutters, gingerbread trim, a tin-roof and, they thought, maybe, a few cats and a chicken. "Not much help," I told them, "that only leaves about three-quarters of the houses in Key West to check out."

About one-half hour later we stumbled upon their inn after cruising almost every street in Old Town. Their description was fairly accurate, missing the bull's-eye by only a cat's hair; no cats were in attendance that morning. These guys were ecstatic and exhausted.

Thrilled that we had finally found the place, they started to leave my cab when Gary stopped and leaned back into my taxi and asked if I could come back and get them around five o'clock that afternoon. A sheepish smile appeared as he casually mentioned to me, "I seem to vaguely remember parking a car somewhere."

Sweet dreams, ya'll.

BEWARE OF PALE PEOPLE CARRYING LUGGAGE

The past three weeks have delivered to Key West a weather triad that is unusual and unexpected. We've experienced three consecutive cold fronts in as many weeks, causing locals to pull out an extra blanket and don sweaters and sweatshirts.

This is February weather and pretty unusual for this time of the year. But, as the expression goes, (and I'll paraphrase a bit), "Stuff Happens!"

We locals know that Key West is not the tropics, but the sub-tropics; we do, in fact, get seasonal changes in weather. Foliage and flowers come and go, as do different species of birds and fish. Our free-range chickens and osprey are year-round dwellers, while our eagles, hawks, wrens and snowbirds like to travel around a bit.

But let us examine, if we may, one of the strangest birds to visit the Keys. An unforgiving bird. A bird that searches far and wide for sunny skies and balmy breezes. A bird whose first call upon alighting on our less-then-tropical coral-rock home sounds something like, "What the hell is this? It's freezing!"

That would be the call of the Overcoated-Pale-Skinned-Luggage-Carrying-Cuckoo, or O.P.S.L.C.C.. This bird is usually of Northern or Midwestern origins and has flown upwards of one, two, or even three thousand circuitous miles before finally roosting in Paradise.

Tedious flight patterns from New York to Chicago to Miami to Key West rack up the air miles, but tend to ruffle feathers as well.

The eating habits of the O.P.S.L.C.C. are also significantly challenged. A diet of salted nuts and alcohol adds to the diminished mental acuity these birds find themselves left with when they eventually nestle into the back seat of my cab for the final leg of their journey.

Grumbling to the tunes of Jimmy Buffett from my radio, most 'get over it' by the time we arrive at their boudoir of choice, with the realization that chilly though we may be, it's probably the warmest spot in the country.

I always try to break the ice (no pun intended) with the question, "Where are you from?" I receive answers such as, Sioux Falls, or Chicago, or Pittsburgh. Followed up by, "And how cold was it when you left?" For most, those questions are the only reality check needed, and the remnants of their frozen tundra syndrome melt considerably.

I always add that these cold spells do not last long, and that hopefully, given a day or two, the sun will shine and the air will be warm once again.

Hopefully! But a word of caution: if the sun does not shine this week, beware of pale people carrying luggage.

BEHIND DOOR NUMBER ONE

The lady stood quietly, her eyes rotating slowly from left to right, taking in the whole scene before her, and scratching her head in confusion. She was a well-dressed, not quite matronly, woman who'd found herself in the unfortunate position of having stumbled into the wrong public restroom, this one being at the Key West International Airport.

She was standing behind a man who was standing in front of the urinal taking care of, and minding, his own business. His back was turned towards her and he was unaware of her presence. As he zipped up and turned to leave, he found himself face-to-face with the woman. He stopped dead. She, recovering her sense of direction, and recognizing a men's room when she saw one, held her head up high and said, "Well, yes, one of us seems to have picked the wrong door and I do hope it was not me. Why don't I go out and check?"

She turned, our eyes met, and she smiled at me as I held the door for her. Then she was gone.

It was, I admit, a gracious exit, and the woman had shown a good degree of ingenuity in removing herself from a potentially uncomfortable situation. Just like magic: now you see me, now you don't. She deserved a round of applause for her performance, and when I left the restroom, I looked around, but had no success in finding her.

The luck of the draw, however, put her at the terminal's sliding doors and looking for a taxi, just as my cab moved to the head of the line.

"Taxi, ma'am?"

"Why yes," she responded, and then added, "Oh, goodness," when she realized she and I had just met in the men's room.

I took her luggage and escorted her to my cab, loading the bag before asking her destination. "Oh, Toronto would be nice," she laughed, kidding about the encounter.

Her name was Betty, she was a physician, and taught at a medical school. She was down from Canada for five days for a convention being held at The Casa Marina hotel.

"Actually, this is not my first strange encounter in a men's room," she told me. "I seem to wander about a bit when I have things on my mind. My husband calls me the absent-minded-professor."

We were approaching the stop sign on Atlantic Boulevard, at the foot of the White Street Pier, when Betty asked if I would mind turning around and going back to the airport.

"No problem. Did you forget something?" I asked.

"Yes, as a matter of fact, I did. The airline misplaced a piece of luggage, and my husband was checking on it. I'm afraid I forgot both it and my husband." Betty and I laughed all the way back to the airport.

I dropped her off, and never did get to meet her spouse. I do hope he has a sense of humor at least half as good as hers.

WEATHER OR NOT

Key West was experiencing one of the few winter cold fronts that was able to press its way all the way down to the Southernmost Point. As the front came through, the winds picked up impressively, and the temperature dropped to 52 degrees, near frigid by Key West standards.

The streets were busy with quivering tourists, sweatshirt-swaddled and cranky at the turn of the weather. Bars overflowed with people huddled together seeking communal warmth, and commiserating with each other about their lack of luck in picking the coldest week of the season to be here on vacation. The street people, the homeless, the indigent, hid in doorways or the lee side of structures, seeking invisibility and protection from the gusty air. They cloaked themselves with blankets and layers of clothing, insulation from the world as well as the wind. Our free-range chickens hunkered down in roosting places, tucked into the protective arms of banyan or gumbo-limbo trees.

Dogs sniffed the cool air with surprised consternation, and rolled into themselves dreaming of summertime frolics, and twitching at tropical, canine poltergeists.

Two women, both wearing one-size-fits-all bikini tops, short-shorts and flip-flops, waved to me from the front of one of Duval Street's watering holes. They were clutching each other, arms entangled, their bodies protectively close. A beach bag in one hand and a liquid libation in the other confirmed the story that spilled out of the couple after they got into my taxi.

In unison they bombarded me with, "What happened to the weather? This is Key West. It's supposed to be sunny and hot, sand, palm trees, 'the Sunshine State,' and instead, it's freezing!" This was all said at just a shade under a shout.

Mary-Marie and her sister JoAnne were huddled into a corner of the back seat of my taxi, and while I did not think that frostbite would be a problem, I asked them if they would like me to turn the heater on. Overjoyed with this simple pleasure, the women told me that they were first-time visitors to Key West, and had flown in the previous night to a glorious sunset.

Today's beautiful morning had inspired them to try a day at the beach, which proceeded nicely until the weather gods threw them a curve ball. They seemed to take this cold front personally.

"Something always happens when we go away. One year the place we stayed at had a fire, and another time we were snowed in and had to stay at an airport for about 30 hours."

In between sips of their drinks, the ladies grumbled and griped, whined and sniveled about the bad weather and their poor luck and sense of timing. They were cold, tired, grumpy, and slightly intoxicated.

"It's still the warmest spot in the country," I pointed out. They grimaced and glossed over that comment like Chap Stick over cracked lips. I had a feeling that this could turn ugly!

They told me how they left the beach as the weather changed, and had found a bar where everyone was sympathetic to their plight. Locals and other tourists alike bought them a round of drinks and then another, and another. "We met a great crowd of neat people," said Mary-Marie."

"We sure laughed a lot," added her sister.

"So, this was a bad day?" I asked, trying to keep the conversation on the light side. They both gave me dirty looks. So much for keeping it light.

"Hey, for one hundred-fifty bucks a night, $4.00 beers, and a rental car we don't need, the least we want is some warm weather."

The ladies were becoming surly.

Just then a cell phone rang, a musical tone that sounded suspiciously like a computerized version of the William Tell Overture. "Not mine," I chimed in, as the ladies fumbled into their bags, JoAnne finally coming out with the serenading instrument.

"Hi, Mom," the conversation started. Then a few, "Uh-hums," followed by several, "No kiddings," accompanied by a couple of perkier, "greats" and "wonderfuls." The call was ended with an, "I love you," and a, "Bye-bye, now."

"It's 8 degrees and snowing back home in Iowa," offered JoAnne, smiling, as she shared that good news with Mary-Marie. "And she thinks we're really lucky to have picked NOW to be down south." Both women seemed to warm at that good news, and Key West's dip in temperature now did not look all that severe.

As we pulled up to the guest house where the sisters were staying, the two left my cab all the happier from the news they had received from their mom about Jack Frost's arrival back in Iowa, while they vacationed in a much warmer, if not balmy, Key West.

It's all about latitude and attitude. Thanks, Mom!

QUEENS FOR A DAY

I can count the number of "bad" fares that I've had this past year on the fingers of one hand. Only one of those was truly obnoxious, the others were all D.W.I.'s – Dumb While Intoxicated.

My latest close encounter of this kind involved a group of eight extremely bulky gentlemen in their twenties that I picked up at one of the hotels along North Roosevelt Boulevard. They piled in and filled my van from wall to wall. Without exception, these guys were exhibiting symptoms of the "a-drop-too-much-syndrome," showing various stages of the affliction, ranging from giddiness to hostility, and everything in between.

After several attempts to get these fellows to focus on a destination, they were, after all, sitting in a taxi, it was decided unanimously to "Get us to Rumrunners as quickly as you can, or else!

Hearing three or four "faggedabowdit's" bandied about, being an astute cab driver and former New Yorker, I asked, "So, where in New York are you guys from?" I had their full attention now, other than the one passenger who was sleeping in the back seat.

"We're from Far Rockaway, Queens, and how'd ya' know we were New Yorkers?" asked the soberest of the crew.

"My old home town," I explained, adding that I could probably guess what most of them did for a living.

It was not a difficult task to reason that a group of eight burly guys from anywhere in that area of Queens, New York, were either cops or firemen. So, I ventured my guess of firemen, which impressed the hell out of all but one of the boys, who was now becoming a wee bit aggressive and belligerent.

Turning onto Duval Street, he slurred out a question, "Have you come outta the closet yet, pal?"

It wasn't so much the question that ticked me off, as the way this inebriated dope sneered at me while asking it. And, since my sexual proclivity is a personal matter between myself, my maker, and of course my wife, I chose to respond to his question with a question. "You're eight, buff guys from Queens, New York sitting butt to butt, thigh to thigh, one of you is sitting on another's lap, and you're asking me about closets? Puh-lease!"

Tongued-tied and a little too drunk to respond effectively, they spilled out of the cab in front of Rumrunners. Even before I pulled away from them at the curb, I heard one of the group insulting a passing Pedicab Driver, who, in the spirit of things, gave the boys the finger, before peddling off down Duval Street.

POTPOURRI

This past week I had an eclectic mix of passengers in my taxi. Some were nice, some not so nice.

The first was an interesting lady from Pensacola, Florida, whose use of the cliché was abundant. Within the time frame it took to go from one end of Duval Street to the other, she advised me that, "You can't judge a book by its cover. It takes one to know one. That's life. It doesn't get much better than this," and, "You get what you pay for." All of these statements were given in good cheer, and the only note of discontent came when I dropped her off at her guesthouse. "I only wish it was a little bit warmer," she confided.

"You can't always get what you want," I responded. She told me that I was a very wise person. I got the final word in with a parting, "It takes one to know one."

Later that day, I had a whiner from Baltimore, who told me that he'd had a great time in Key West, but then complained all the way to the airport. He bemoaned the rooms being too expensive, the food being less than great and, the final insult, the beer not being cold enough. This man was not a pleasant person to be around. But one of the nice things about driving a pink cab in Key West is that the longest you have to put up with an obnoxious passenger is, at the maximum, about 10 minutes.

I pulled up to the airport's entrance. The Monroe

County Sheriff Department had its post-September 11th security checkpoint in full swing. The whiner was less than pleased, and let out a stream of invectives regarding his valuable time being infringed upon, and that he'd never fly to Key West again, and if there was a train he'd be taking that instead of being subjected to this kind of inconvenience.

A train?

His luggage was an interesting combination. He'd managed to attach a soft suitcase to a hard suitcase, and used clear packing tape to further attach his sneakers to the whole pile that was then attached to a small cart.

"I suppose you want me to open my luggage?" asked the whiner.

The Sheriff's deputy smiled and nodded, and my passenger went ballistic. He was going to report everyone at the airport to someone or other. Needless to say, my tip was history. "Have a nice day."

My favorite of the week was a group of four who flagged me down at Smather's Beach. The group consisted of a bearded man who spoke almost no English and had a patch over one eye, and his female companion, who wore a tiny bikini. This woman had two of the largest, firmest, most well developed...German Shepherds that I have ever seen. (Bet you weren't thinking German Shepherds here.) She told me they were very well-behaved, and well-behaved they were. They hopped into the back seat and made themselves comfortable on the floor, the Shepherds, not the people, and were delightful passengers, making no muss, and no fuss.

The beard and the bikini, though, fought a raging battle all the way to their destination. They shouted and cursed at each other, and upon exiting, left a trail of debris.

The rest of the group left quietly, as they came, licking me as a parting gesture (that's the dogs, not the people).

It just goes to show you, it takes all kinds.

WHAT'S IN A NAME?

Ipicked up a gentleman at the Casa Marina hotel this past week. He wanted to make a quick stop at a guesthouse on Fleming Street, and was then off to the airport.

Nicely dressed and wearing mirrored sunglasses, he looked at me and said, "Well, don't you recognize me?" I looked him over and decided I did not know this man, and I told him so. He stared at me, took his glasses off, and said, "How about now, look familiar?"

Sensing this might be a trick question, I took my time to study him more carefully, and answered with a definitive, "Nope!"

My passenger was now up to the challenge, determined that I recognize him. Truthfully, I did not have the faintest idea who this guy was.

"If I told you that I was the lead singer of a famous rock group, would that help you at all?"

Once again, I gave him a good once over, thinking I might be getting on this guy's nerves. I explained to him that my knowledge of current famous rock groups was extremely limited, and unless he was a Beatle, a Rolling Stone, or a Door, there was little, if any, chance I would recognize him.

To give credit its due, the fellow was not yet ready to throw in the towel. "I'm the lead singer with The Backstreet Boys," he announced.

He smiled at me.

I smiled at him.

Then I asked, "And what was that name again?"

He was a nice young man, and he laughed out loud and told me his group had recently played in Sydney, Australia, and that they were mobbed by fans wherever they went, and needed bodyguards to help them navigate when they went out for a meal.

I told him that Key West is a pretty good town in its dealings with celebrities. Most of us, locals that is, really couldn't care less who he was unless he had something to do with affordable housing or a good meal. (We tend to take our restaurants a bit more seriously than we do our rich and famous.)

After dropping my fare off at the airport, I stopped to tell a couple of cab drivers about my famous fare.

"Yup, lead singer with The Backstreet Boys," I told them.

In unison, their response was, "Who?"

ERNEST'S GHOST

[Editor's note: Every July since 1980, Key West has been the host to a week-long 'Hemingway Days Celebration' to honor of one of its more colorful former residents. Writer, sportsman, drinker, fisherman, the Ernest celebration includes granddaughter Lauren Hemingway's nationally renowned Short Story Writing Contest, a look-alike contest, fishing tournaments, and numerous other contests of male one-upmanship. This column ends with Michael's poem about how Hemingway might feel if his ghost paid a visit to Key West during the celebration that bears his name.]

Hemingway Days roll around in mid-July. We will be inundated with salt-and-pepper hair and beards, khaki shorts, and tall tales. Every third man on the street will look like Ernest just back from a fishing trip off the coast of Cuba. All of them vying for that most exalted of positions, to be the winner of the Hemingway look-a-like contest held at Sloppy Joe's each year.

The following happened during last year's celebration. Ernest Hemingway flagged my cab on Duval Street, by Sloppy Joe's. Actually, three Ernest Hemingways jumped into my back seat and said, "Charterboat Row, and step on it. We've got us a boat to catch."

The three jovial souls were evidently happy as puppies to be:

- in each others' good company,
- en-route to an evening of fishing,
- in Key West for Hemingway Days, and
- feeling no pain.

"So, which one of you gents is the real Ernest Hemingway?" I asked innocently.

I didn't realize it when I asked, but that question started a real tug-o-war. Here were three "Papa" look-a-likes, each trying to convince me that he was the one and only, the real McCoy, the original Ernest Hemingway.

Pulling up to the charterboat fishing docks, I listened to enthusiastic banter about the running of the bulls, Paris in the twenties, lions on safari, drinks and drunks, and boxing and cockfights. How his second wife was the best he ever had, and how he wished he had never looked down the barrel of that damn shotgun.

Finally, out of steam and out of stories, these fine gents looked around and realized that their boat had left without them, and that they would not be catching that "great fish" tonight. They looked at each other, shrugged, then chorused, "Back to Sloppy's!"

Once there, they left my cab and jostled their way back into the bar, waving as the crowd swallowed them. I never did figure out which one was the real Ernest Hemingway.

With this year's festivities fast approaching, I am ready and my list of questions is formidable:

How many books did you write?

What was your first wife's name?

Which street did you live on while in Paris in the 1920's?

This year, I'm going to get it right. As they said on the old TV show, To Tell the Truth, "Will the real Ernest Hemingway please stand up?

ERNEST'S GHOST

Walking up and down the street,
from coast to coast actually,
every third man on the street
is Ernest Hemingway.
Tan shorts, white beard and hair,
an even smile and a willingness
to buy you a beer
or arm-wrestle a bit.

One tells the story
about how the lion almost got him
out on the Veldt, on safari,
but his rifle there on his lap saved him.
Another talks about the Spanish civil war,
and another about the running of the bulls.
All Papa's stories, but which one...
which one is Ernest?
His ghost comes to Key West each year
and walks the streets that he walked
when life was good
and his flesh was real.
He looks for old friends
now dead and earthen
so many years after his own bell tolled.
No one is left to greet him.

And if someone was left
how would they know him?
Pick him out of the line-up,
ask him to write something, prove who he was?

But this year I spotted him.
Ernest was standing in front of his old haunt
with dozens of other Ernest look-a-likes walking by.

Papa's ghost, just looking into Sloppy's, shaking his head.
No beer in his hand.
No tall tales.
Only Ernest standing there,
mouth open, shaking his head.

GETTING STUCK IN KEY WEST

Several weeks ago I met Janice and Paul, both bankers, who said they were down from Miami for a few days of R & R, and wanted to find someplace local, and clean, to get a tattoo. These two nice people were clearly in party mode and feeling little or no pain, so I good-naturedly explained that there were no tattoo parlors directly in Key West. The closest was a short cab ride away on Stock Island. "Let's do it," they sang out in unison, and away we went in search of the perfect tattoo.

Janice wanted something small and pretty, maybe a butterfly, down near the base of her spine. She wiggled around a bit and pointed to the general area of her intended canvas (gee, I love this job), and explained that she had to have it in a discrete area because her father is very old-fashioned and would be embarrassed if he knew that his daughter had a tattoo anywhere on her body, much less her chosen spot. And the financial institution where she and Paul worked would probably be pretty ticked off, as well.

Paul was thinking along similar lines and pondered a snake, or maybe "MOM" surrounded by hearts on his thigh or buttock, hidden from his stodgy bosses whom he thought might "freak" if his personal artwork showed.

"Are the needles clean? Do they sterilize them, or what? What if the artist screws up the picture?" Janice was starting to get a little nervous about the adventure as we pulled up in front of one of Stock Island's finest tattoo emporiums.

They both left the cab, promising to call when they were finished, so that I could see their finished products.

But the end of my shift came and went without that call, so I never did get to see exactly where they both got their tattoos.

I smile when I think about it. Bankers in ivory towers, computing loan rates and examining balance sheets... I wonder what they're sitting on, besides their chairs?

Maybe a snake, a butterfly or "MOM."

JOHNNY B. GONE

The slender man with hair the color of coal flagged my taxi early one morning. Dressed all in black, he had Johnny Cash at Folsom Prison look about him. He was carrying a guitar case that was slung casually over one shoulder, and a duffel bag hung from the other. He was jumping up and down trying to get my attention, which he did, and I pulled over to the curb. I hopped out of my cab and was walking around to open the trunk so that he could deposit his belongings when, in a blink, Johnny was gone. Then I heard a door slam. Johnny had thrown his stuff into the back seat, then elbowed himself a place to sit, and was waiting for me when I climbed back in behind the wheel. He had wide eyes and a smile that could have been painted on, and he spoke rapidly in short bursts, and asked me if I could find a Western Union office for him.

"Money's comin' and I can't wait." He told me that he had had enough of Key West, and was waiting for some money to be wired to him so that he could "get outta town."

The story unfolded. Johnny and his guitar had made the trip from Los Angeles, and had been visiting Key West hoping to find a music venue to showcase his talents. Not only was he an accomplished musician, singer, songwriter and playwright, he told me, he was also a stand-up comedian.

The man sounded like he could handle as full a plate as the next guy, but Johnny had a nervous energy about him, and he sat up on the edge of his seat as he talked to me. He was moving back and forth as if he were in a rocking chair, and his hands were in constant motion, either cracking his knuckles, or kneading his fingers. I wasn't exactly sure what this guy's problem was but, "Man on the verge of a breakdown" was a passing thought.

It was a beautifully lazy Key West morning. The quietly subdued colors of winter had exploded into spectacular reds and yellows and pinks. The canopy of Royal Poinciana was blooming to form a vibrant orange umbrella that would soon cover a goodly chunk of the city. Migrating birds sang and the prevailing winds slowly started to swing to the south. A day unfolding at its own pace. Paradise, for most of us.

"What's with this place?" Johnny wanted to know. "Everything moves in slow motion. How can you stand it?"

My response, "Slow is good," did little to endear myself to him.

His rocking increased, and his eyes grew wider as he spoke. I was starting to get somewhat nervous myself.

"Coffee, I can't find a good cuppa coffee. I've tried six or seven places today, and can't find anything other than that Cuban stuff. You people ever hear of Starbuck's, huh?"

Ahh, coffee. Johnny's drug of choice. He was caffeinated to the max, and was revolving at 78 rpm's in a 33 1/3 rpm town.

En route to the Western Union office we found ourselves behind a Conch Tour Train, one of those caterpillar-type vehicles that crawls through our streets filled with sightseers, with top speeds of about six miles an hour.

Johnny's agitation level elevated in direct proportion to the decreased speed of the traffic and snail's pace of our own progress. "I...can't...stand...this," he almost whimpered, and some part of me did connect with the agony Johnny was experiencing.

We reached our destination, and Johnny got out and asked me to wait for him. When he got back into my taxi he was a very much relieved person. His money had been wired to him, he had guessed the secret password, and Western Union had delivered his cash, which was his passport out of purgatory.

"So, what time does your plane leave?" I asked.

"Oh, I'm not flying," was his immediate response, as he upped his rocking speed a notch. "I'm taking the Greyhound."

Oh, boy!

I expect that two days hence, somewhere around Iowa City, and surrounded by newly seeded cornfields, the rocking will reach critical mass, and will start to become a problem. Unless, of course, there's a Starbuck's handy.

SOUTHERN BELLE

The couple in my cab had several stops to make, and the tall woman with exceptionally blond hair tucked under a floppy straw hat asked me, in a deep southern drawl, if I could make the rounds of several stores with them. They had a long list of presents to buy. These seemed like nice people, visiting Key West for a little rest, relaxation, and shopping. He was a jovial type, energetic, and deeply tanned. A golfer's tan. His wife was somewhat subdued, but pleasant, in a "Tara, I'll never go hungry again" sort of way. She had a complexion of bone china.

The first stop on their list was the Key Lime Shoppe at Green and Elizabeth Streets. "We're shipping a whole key lime pie back home to my mama," the woman told me. "Won't she be surprised?"

What a nice thing to do, I thought, as we pulled up to the curb. The man got out and his wife said, "I'll just wait here and keep this nice man company, dear." He nodded and turned to leave, but called out to me before entering the store, "Anything I can get for you?" It was a generous offer, but I shook my head no.

I turned to face the woman and we exchanged some small talk. She looked at me for a minute, then leaned forward and softly asked me in a voice dripping with brown sugar and pralines, "Would y'all like to bite my thigh?"

The 'thigh' word was presented in a stretched out, painfully delicious, Belle of the South inflection.

I looked over my shoulder to the doorway of the Key Lime Shoppe, exhaled an "Oh, boy," and hoped for her husband's rapid return. Attempting to re-route the course of this conversation, I disarmingly asked, "So, have you two been to the sunset celebration yet?"

She peered at me, still waiting for my answer. Sensing no wiggle room or simple avoidance to the question, I responded, "Another generous offer, thanks, but I'll pass."

Her husband came bouncing back into my taxi, and we were off to the next in their series of stops. At each store, the woman would stay in my cab and keep me company while her husband did the shopping.

At a jewelry store, I was offered a breast to go along with the aforementioned thigh. At Keno's Sandals, I was presented with a display of moistened lips. As we waited for her husband in front of Commotion, a clothing store in a building that once was a famous bordello, a whispered request involving spanking unfolded, and while that did garner my attention, yet again, I passed.

Around the corner from Sloppy Joe's a suggestion was made that would have left the Marquis de Sade quivering like a bowl of J-E-L-L-O. The lady was persistent and I was perspiring.

The cab was rapidly filling up with shopping bags full of goodies, and I was beginning to feel like the mouse that had been left alone with the cat for too long. This lady was bad, and "thanks, but no thanks," was falling upon a deaf libido. Her husband came back with yet another armful of purchases, and announced the shopping trip to be both successful and complete.

My audible sigh of relief as we headed back to the couple's hotel caused the man to ask me, "Has she been hitting on you?" He didn't wait for my answer, for which I was thankful, but he continued with, "It's a game she plays. She thinks it's great fun. She does it everywhere we go. Sometimes it gets embarrassing."

Talk about an understatement.

My eyeballs were still rolling around in my head when we reached their destination and parted company. As they left my cab, the woman leaned in through my window and winked at me long and slow before following her husband, laden with packages, back into their hotel.

She had toyed with me like the spider did the fly, enticing me into her tangled web. And I wasn't sure whether I felt flattered by the invitations, annoyed by the concept, or relieved to be done with it.

The one thing I was sure of was that I needed a cold shower.

A SIREN'S CALL

It was a cool, overcast Key West day. February can be like that. The woman I picked up in my cab early Monday morning wanted to go to the beach. "No swimming for me," she explained, "but it's just gray enough to be beautiful."

I agreed, and suggested the beach at Fort Zachary Taylor State Park. We pulled into a nearly deserted parking area, and I stopped the cab as close to the beach as I could maneuver.

Somewhere in the distance, opera was playing. We heard a voice like Maria Callas', the quintessential soprano, singing loud and rich and clear. The voluptuous voice appeared to be rolling in from the ocean. We listened for a moment to be sure of the sounds that we were hearing. My passenger, Mona, an adventurous matron from Mamaroneck, New York, and I looked at each other and then shrugged. We both knew we were on a mission.

"Park this thing and leave the meter running," she said with a conspiratorial twinkle in her eye.

I backed up and parked nearest to the path that led to the beach. We walked toward the sea and Maria Callas. The sand was nearly empty, not a beach day by many Floridians' standards. Two children played at the water's edge, their mother huddled into the warmth of a heavy sweatshirt that was pulled up to, and over, her nose so that only her eyes and hair were exposed to the

chilly easterly breeze. The children laughed as they wad-
dled, crab-like, along the coarse and rocky sand, immune
to the stone and coral sharpness beneath them.

And still Maria Callas sang.

Mona and I followed the aria and walked along a
thin dirt path that wiggled its way atop a small bluff that
overlooked the beach. Whispers of sunlight occasionally
broke through the leaden sky and cast long silver fingers
of light across a slate gray seascape.

At the far end of the beach lies a rock jetty that
embraces the entrance to Key West Harbor. It is a
favorite spot for brides and grooms to exchange their
wedding vows, with the backdrop of the southernmost
sunset behind them. This harbor is the funnel through
which giant cruise ships and tiny sailboats enter the city
from both the Atlantic Ocean and the Gulf of Mexico. We
saw no one standing upon the jetty, but the beautiful
melody seemed to rise from the very rock itself. We quietly approached the lip of the jetty and peered over the
edge with hopes of finding the source of the wonderful
sounds.

Standing with her back to us was our diva. Long
black locks of hair tumbled down her back, the wind
throwing it around carelessly, as she stood with her
arms upraised to the sky. She sang to the heavens and
to the sea. It was magic that erupted from her as she
beautifully, and flawlessly, projected an exquisite operat-
ic voice out over the ocean. She was also stark naked,
with a pile of clothing and a bright pink towel at her feet.
Her figure was as full and round as her voice, and jiggled
as her siren's song swelled from her and was cast onto
the rolling waters.

Mona and I turned and left as quietly as we had
come. As we drove out of the park we concluded that the
mysterious chanteuse was so fully engrossed in her performance that she never knew that we had been eaves-
dropping. Back on Duval Street, we said our good-byes,
each of us with high praise and a new respect for opera

in its *au natural* form.

Two hours later I received a call again to Fort Zachary Taylor State Park. It was noontime and the sun had broken through the overcast sky, and people were on the beach taking advantage of what appeared to be the makings of a beautiful day.

In the parking lot, hailing my cab, stood a robust, full-figured woman with a pink towel rolled tightly under one arm. Her long black hair flogged back and forth in the still-brisk breeze.

A single word reverberated within me, *Encore.*

Angelina's Pizza
208 Duval Street

III

The River of Duval

*Many of my vignettes about life in and about the streets of
Key West pass directly in front of the cinemascopic big
screen of my taxi's window. One would need to be
blindfolded not to witness the humor, drama and joy that
are so abundant here. While I cruise the coast to coast
ribbon of Duval Street that ties the Atlantic Ocean to the
Gulf of Mexico, I am always amazed and entertained.
The people who walk and inhabit this street are an
ensemble of characters rich in texture and flavor, seasoned
to perfection with laughter, pathos and salt air.
I hardly know which to sample first.*

BETTE MIDLER MEETS CARY GRANT

Nervously, hands twitching as if he'd had too much coffee, the young man with wide, wild eyes climbed the three steps to the patio's verandah. He put his bag down, stretched, raised his arms and beat his chest, doing a pretty good Tarzan wail, "Ahyaaaaa eyyaaaaaaa ahyaaaaaa."

His abrupt serenade left him isolated from the rest of the café. Those at nearby tables shifted their presence to vacant seats further from the vortex.

He quieted and went to sit down at the small bistro table, first brushing crumbs from the polished tabletop, and stooping even further to flick a small piece of pastry from the cushioned seat. Sparrow-like birds darted around his feet, feasting on his generosity.

Well-dressed and carefully groomed, he appeared harmless, only his entrance a testament to something not quite right.

The waitress came and he ordered a cheese-filled delicacy and something to drink, and fussed with his napkin and tableware, arranging and rearranging them while he waited.

He had a great conversation going on with himself, swinging between a Limey accent, early Cary Grant, and a Brooklyn-twanged Bette Midler.

"Tea would be nice," said the divine Miss M.

"Oh, do allow me to order you some," was the singular response. And so this one-person conversation continued.

A nicely dressed couple in tourist garb tentatively sat at an adjacent table, not yet aware that they had just entered "stage right." It took them but a moment to discern they'd picked the wrong table, and they tried without much success to avoid eye contact with their neighbor.

"Hey!—How ya doing?—Great day!—Where ya from?—Stayin' in town?—How long?—I'm goin' to rent a boat—Take a trip around South America—China maybe, or Korea —Catch a Great White Shark when I'm out there—I'm really wealthy, legally wealthy—All of my papers say so—But the court has it all screwed up—Say, what do you do for a living?"

It was one continuous run-on sentence, without taking a breath.... Then silence.

The couple smiled at the man and got up and left, almost stumbling down the steps to the safety of Duval Street.

More silence.

Bette Midler leaned over to Cary Grant and said, "Dirtbags."

The sparrows waited patiently for dessert.

SPAGHETTI WESTERN

S weet rain fell, delicious offerings to a parched earth. Raindrops the size of cherries splashed and sizzled on steaming sidewalks, sending columns of mist spiraling skyward.

Casual Duval Street strollers looked up to the heavens, cast a sigh of relief, then ran like hell as drenching sheets of water, a Niagara of rain, saturated the crowd. The storm crept in from the south and was over the horizon in a flash. A gray mist in the distance at one moment, it silently stole across the Florida Straits, and, as it touched land, its fuse lit, ignited a cacophony of raucous explosions.

Torrents fell from the heavens as the storm's fury flared. The lightening, bright and immediate, framed the kettledrum rhythm. Clouds boiled in a gun-metal gray sky, the air hummed with electricity. The streets flooded. Water flowed from curb to curb, cars leaving wakes like motorboats as they passed.

People took shelter in front of gift shops and galleries, bars and restaurants, in doorways and under awnings. Storefronts were crowded with afternoon window shoppers waiting out the deluge as the potbellied canvas overflowed with rain. Strangers huddled against each other and pressed tightly to plate glass, hoping to find solace from the soggy day.

Two hens, brown feathers matted flat from the

rain, bobbed and clucked their way towards a clutch of people standing under the canopy of a restaurant. The people watched as the hens stood before them being pelted by the rain. Slowly, a universal consciousness moved the crowd. Like the Red Sea for Moses, the throng parted for the two hens

Moments later the storm had passed as suddenly as it had arrived, and the huddled crowd slipped away in ones and twos, ultimately leaving just the two hens by themselves. The sun had reappeared, but the chickens stood their ground. Passersby looked at them, and the chickens looked back.

Suddenly, the doors to the restaurant swung open and a waiter appeared with a water gun in his hands. Chasing and squirting the birds as he ran, it was a Key West Spaghetti Western amid squawks and the flapping of wings.

The chickens scurried and scattered and the street was alive with frantic activity. The waiter stopped and laughed, blew across the tip of his faux smoking gun, then returned to the restaurant.

A slow moment passed quietly and, like the tide, the hens returned, pecking and picking at delicious delicacies scattered curbside by the rain.

The River of Duval Street flowed by.

SPRING BREAK

The rites of spring came early to Key West this year, with the first wave of spring-breakers showing up at our hotels and guesthouses in early March, flocking like lemmings do to the great cliffs. Their purpose is the same as it has always been: the four B's of Beer, Booze, Better weather, and Beautiful bodies.

The streets crackled with testosterone and estrogen as hormones worked overtime and were only subtly subdued by the cooler than anticipated weather. Great pods of students passed each other, nodding and checking out physical attributes. Heads turned, eyes met, smiles and names were exchanged.

Also visiting Key West were several thousand participants of Daytona's Bike Week that coincided with spring's eternal Dating Game, the cooler than usual weather drawing the beer-bellied and bandana'd bikers to the southernmost city, as well.

Rounding out the mix was Key West's eclectic allotment of cruise ship passengers, numbering approximately 4,000 each day, from all over the country. On any day one could view crewcuts from Detroit, polyestered seniors from South Bend, and sophisticated bons vivants from Boothbay Harbor.

Mix into this concoction white-booted shrimpers, holed-up in a safe harbor from the near gale-force winds that had prevented their boats from venturing out to sea.

Throw in a hobo or two, or three, seeking a warmer clime in which to hide their homelessness, and the tropical cocktail that we know as spring break was ready and set to go.

This particular morning most eyes were directed to the skies, gray and ominous and showing scant signs of the much-coveted sunshine and warmth that all were seeking. Few saw the local resident who peddled by on his pink bicycle wearing tights and a lace tutu, a cigar tucked below his mustachioed lip. Few saw the tiny dog with toenails painted bright red, who lifted his leg and shot a steady stream onto the wing-tipped shoes of a man wearing plaid shorts and a tee shirt that announced, "Beer: The Breakfast of Champions," and few saw the woman with bright orange hair arguing with her mirror image reflecting back from a storefront's plate glass window.

The street moved in slow motion. The crowd and the traffic were in sync with each other, orchestrated to the rhythm of the morning, and moving like a ballet. People pirouetted and spun in conjunction with sights and sounds, as motorcycles vied with pedicabs for prime space, and Elvis look-a-likes wandered past the Heartbreak Hotel.

The woman with the orange hair sat down on the steps in front of a bookstore. She huddled into herself, her arms protectively wrapped from shoulder to shoulder, and slowly rocked back and forth. She wore a thin white blouse, one sleeve torn and dirty. Behind her in the store window was perched a cat, a gray striped tabby. The woman had a cup and a sign placed on the ground before her. The sign simply said, PLEASE, in large block letters. The cup was empty.

Her loud hair, tousled by the wind and gnarly from grit, flagged across her face and caused her to grimace as she repeatedly tried to brush it back behind her ears. She and the cat watched the flow of people, their eyes and heads following as people passed, and then back again, as another group entered their lines of vision.

They sat like that, the woman and the cat, and watched. No one stopped to put money in her cup or to talk to her. Not one person looked at her. No one stopped to look at the cat, either. They were invisible.

The sun finally poked through the clouds and the energy and pace of the street increased rapidly as if the people, cars, bikes and scooters all sensed urgency in the day.

The woman sat quietly, tears now running down her cheeks, as the crowd sped by her. Her eyes no longer tracked them as her tears spilled and pooled.

The cat looked at the woman, placed its paw to the window, and meowed.

AT THE AIDS MEMORIAL

The River of Duval has many tributaries along its slender ribbon that ties the Gulf of Mexico to the Atlantic Ocean. Each adds vibrant life and colorful stories that unfold before me each day.

Tales of loving and living, joy and sorrow, life and death, highlight the diorama that is Key West, with its vast diversity in social, economic and cultural conditions. The city's official motto of "One Human Family" focuses on our similarities instead of our differences.

The following, originally written as a poem, depicts my observations over a three day period while passing the Key West AIDS Memorial, at the foot of the White Street Pier.

DAY ONE: In the early evening, the sun has descended, tucked into its turquoise bed to sleep until the morning's tide awakens it. It is quiet now at the White Street pier. Worshipers of the departing sun have slowly drifted into the ebb and flow of the street, and are gently swept away. Palm fronds crackle in the breeze, electric with the current of the wind. A lone runner slows, then jogs in place, in cadence to the rhythm of the words etched in marble before him: *'Tis better to have loved and lost than never to have loved at all.*

Tennyson's words stir the jogging figure, and he moves slowly past the sleeping: Rawls, Bishop, Morales, Kelly, Vonner... hundreds and hundreds of names; brother, sister, son, daughter, husband, wife, lover, friend. It is always sunset at the AIDS Memorial on White Street.

DAY TWO: A solitary figure stands before the marble plaques, studying each column, looking for a familiar name. He moves cautiously along the length of the Memorial, feeling perhaps, that too quick a movement will carry him past an old friend or relative. He circles the many names, confused at first, then, hands on hips, stops, leans forward and nods. He stands quietly for a moment, solemn and meditative. A tropical breeze, throwing hair across his brow, breaks the spell and causes the man to shake his head. Wiping a tear from his eye, he silently turns, leaving the stones alone...again.

A lone black dog wanders in off the beach and walks the length of the Memorial as if looking for a name. He lays down where the man had stood just a moment ago, and rests his head on the cool marble at the foot of the White Street pier.

DAY THREE: A tourist-laden Conch Train stops at the corner of White and Atlantic Streets, announcing the prominence of the White Street Pier, and with a "ding-ding" chiming, it moves away, with no mention of the AIDS Memorial. On the sand beyond, a Yoga class practices, a man in tattered shorts rummages through a garbage can looking for buried treasure.

A little boy rolls a fuzzy, chartreuse tennis ball across a marble tome by Gibran, which is etched in the memorial's stone. He jumps with joy as his Sheltie pup runs to scoop it away.

No one person greets the black stones. No one bows their head today, or utters a condolence or smiles at a memory.

It's lonely at the Memorial when no one stops to remember.

A KNOCK AT HEAVEN'S GATE

I picked up a fare this week on one of the narrow lanes of Key West's Bahama Village.

An afternoon thunderstorm had left the streets pooled with water. The tropical sun evaporated the deluge's remnants in ribbons of mist that rose from cracked pavement. Trees, heavy with the Rain God's offerings, deposited droplets to the ground in melancholy rhythm. A gecko clung precariously to a Royal Poinciana tree, waiting patiently for a snack to pass by, while a fresh layer of red flowers, loosened by the storm, blanketed the roadway with a regal coverlet. Chickens pecked, cats scratched, and dogs lazed away the hot, hazy day of a Key West summer.

It was a scene from a postcard of a Caribbean Isle somewhere beyond the horizon, a village moving in slow motion, in sync with the tropical heat and adhering to the rules of the soaring thermometer and escalating humidity.

While I waited for my fare to emerge from his house, I took in this scene and felt almost transported to a different place, my windshield a cinemascopic rendering of paradise.

The cab door opened and broke the spell. Artis jumped in. "Hey Mon, can you take me to that bank out there by Flagler Avenue? I have to get my paycheck cashed."

Artis is an energetic man with smooth cocoa skin plus the clearest eyes and disposition I've encountered in a long while. He was from the "Islands," and the lilt to his voice was musical. He fit into my postcard scene just perfectly.

I told him that the same bank he wanted to go to had a branch much closer then the one out on Flagler, but he was adamant that the one he said was the one he wanted to go to.

"Mon, the people out there treat me nice. They know who I am! The people in the other bank office, they don't treat me nice."

He explained that whenever he went to the closer bank, they were never courteous; they watched him like he was going to steal their pens or try to get a glimpse of where they hid the keys to the safe. They didn't know who he was.

Artis is very philosophical in his opinions. In his 30-something years of age he has managed to sort through the intolerance and ignorance of discrimination, and bring it down to its lowest common denominator: Self.

"I can't change them, but I do know who I am. When you know who you are, you are closer to the Gates of Heaven."

What a wise man.

MEMORIES

M y last fare of the day, a charming seventy-something lady from South Carolina, sits quietly observing the gentle street we are driving on, and I comment about the library and its Palm Garden as we pass.

My windows are open to the fragrant, early-evening scents of night-blooming jasmine and frangipani, delicate, delicious floral flavors, tasty morsels for the senses. I then point to a sparkling conch house: the house made famous by the *This Old House* television program. The woman nods her head as I announce the various sights, but as we arrive at the corner of William and Fleming Streets, she shouts, "STOP!" She scares the daylights out of me, and I do indeed stop, slamming on my brakes in order to discover what my passenger's sense of urgency is attempting to convey.

"What, what, what?" repeated in rapid succession is all that I can summon.

"Wherever is that music coming from?" asks my passenger in an euphoric drawl.

Ah, the music!

Next to us on the corner stands a large, pale, coral pink structure, taller than most of the neighboring buildings. Its rooftop is turreted on three sides to resemble a medieval castle. The stained-glass windows, though, project the image of a house of worship. Paint, chipped and peeling, and window frames decaying under a relentless Key West sun, leave only one's imagination to help proclaim its once-proud bearing.

The windows are tilted open to allow in the soft tropical breeze, and let the spirited music loft out as well. Sweet, sweet music. Music for the soul. Taxicab-stopping music. We are both hooked!

I pull abreast of the old weathered building, and my passenger and I exit my cab.

Several people passing by stop to listen to the rhythm of the saints, as the woman soloist at the altar holds up her hands in a greeting.

The church, which has a mostly black congregation, is filled with people. The children sit or stand holding a parent's hand; there is not much fidgeting taking place here. The men in sports jackets and suits, some wearing starched white shirts, several with neckties, glisten with sweat as the heat takes its toll, even so late in the day. The women are mostly wearing polite dresses; a few with hats add a dignified appearance to the meeting. Ushers and usherettes, white gloved and proper, survey the congregation, waiting to be of assistance if the need occurs.

The building rocks with the music of the Lord. It rolls with old-time religion. The pastor, a diminutive woman wearing a bright red dress, sings out sweet and clear, her voice resonating throughout the building. Her music draws "Hallelujahs!" and "Sing it, sister," from many in the large, high-ceilinged chapel, and a few clap with her as she sings.

The room is touched by love. The room is also touched by pain. A young woman, her hair set in perfect cornrows, sobs audibly, adding a touch of melancholy to the scene.

My passenger leans close and softly tells me that this reminds her of home when she was a little girl. And of church picnics, and shiny patent-leather shoes. "Folks took religion seriously when I was growing up," she adds.

The pastor's hymn comes to an end, and the congregation, along with the group gathered by the open windows and doors, applaud in appreciation.

The preacher leads smoothly into her sermon, which is one of love and inclusion, not of fire and brimstone. She talks to each and every person listening, and she talks also to my passenger. The woman from South Carolina excuses herself and tells me that she just wants to pop her head into the church for a minute and look around.

But I think that I knew that her childhood memories were flowing back to her, as they often do for many of us when something triggers a moment from years passed. She was perhaps remembering wearing her Sunday best, and then, afterwards, her family and her young friends at a church picnic, complete with fried chicken, potato salad, and a gentle reminder that "the biscuits are in the oven, and warmin'."

A minute passes quickly and she returns. "I think I will just stay here now," the woman says. "You can feel the spirit in this church." And you could, even from the seat of my cab as I drove away, you could.

GLADLY THIS CROSS I BEAR

S toically exuding religiosity, the large man bears his cross well. His beard, a salt-and-pepper confetti of confusion, tumbles down his barrel chest and comes to rest atop a more ample belly. He walks the length of Duval Street, wearing white robes and floppy sandals, his feet darkened with street grit. Hoisted upon his shoulder is a symbol larger than the man himself. It is a shimmering metallic announcement that catches the sun's rays, along with your attention, as he passes. It stands well over six-feet tall and spreads an ungainly six-feet across. A crucifix.

He treads the street, the hand-lettered epitaph upon his cross changing daily with messages from his soul. People give him a wide berth; he's a modern-day Messiah walking upon water salted with sinners and saints.

This day his pronouncement reads, *The Cross is lighter, the burden remains.* Appropriately, his words are colored bright pink, adding a Fellini-esque quality to the scene. The proselytizer speaks to no one. His eyes are alive with energy, radiant beacons wordlessly preaching doom and salvation.

He stops in front of St. Paul's Church, its stuccoed walls soaring high above Duval Street. Majestic stained-glass windows, open to catch the breeze, allow strains of organ music to perfume the air.

Standing motionless in front of the whitewashed church, his body poised before the steps of the sanctuary, and clutching his prophecy snugly against his body, the man in monk's robes is transfixed.

A blink could transport you to another time, another place. Closed eyes bring visions of throngs of people along a narrow, winding street, watching a man in robes carrying a similar burden made of wood. You could see the crown of thorns, taste the blood, sense the faith and despair.

"Mister, you dropped your banana."

The spell was broken. The man in white robes, hair flagging in the soft wind, looked down at the boy of six or seven who, with his parents, had just left the comfort of the church. The boy held in one hand a banana that had slipped from beneath the folds of the man's garment and landed at his feet. The boy's other hand tugged gently at his robes.

"Want your banana, mister?" the boy asked once more, holding the bright, yellow fruit higher still.

The prophet reached down and took the banana, gently touched the boy's head, and smiled. As he turned to go, he hefted his burden securely back upon his shoulders.

"Hey, mister," the boy called out again. "You didn't say thank you."

The man in white robes stepped gently upon the flowing River of Duval, and never looked back.

A PROPER SUNDAY DINNER

W hat a charming elderly lady she appeared to be, right out of a Norman Rockwell illustration. Gray wispy hair, light and fluffy, waving in the slight cool breeze of a delicate Key West Sunday morning. Her dress, white with tropical promise, and covered with lime green flowers, was perfection in little more than a size three, or five, at most.

She wore old jewelry on her twig-like wrists and fingers. Dark tarnished gold, belonging to aged hands, these rings and bracelets had been with her, I am sure, for most of the years of her life. And pearls of course, at her ears and neck, telling all.

She floated into the little French café, peering here and there, weighing the pros and cons of polished tables against somewhat littered floors. You could hear a pensive "hmmm," almost, but not quite, curtained by the palest of pink lipstick

Her companion, her grandson or great-nephew, fully adult, yet awkward in her presence, walked a few paces behind, caution in his steps. Not wanting to be far enough away to hurt her feelings, if she even noticed, he did not want to be close enough to be included in whatever scene was unfolding. Perhaps he was slightly embarrassed by her antiquity.

Nodding now, she decided this place would do. "I'm trying to find you a proper Sunday dinner," she sharply announced. Her strength of voice burst forth, vibrant and resonating with authority.

"What?" he said, closing the gap between them now that she had commanded.

"A proper Sunday dinner," she repeated, sterner than before, turning heads and stopping half-lifted cups of coffee. He glanced about, embarrassed, knowing that the small café had focused all its attention on the both of them.

Once more, even louder, "Maybe here we can find you a proper Sunday dinner." Her lips curled to a knowing smile. She was aware and well satisfied that he hadn't had a "proper" Sunday dinner since he left home, probably Atlanta or Savanna. Her lilt admitted bravely to her southern heritage.

They both stood quietly. Only their heads turned to gaze slowly upon the treasures the elderly lady had found, to look at shelf upon shelf of beignets, croissants and brioche, stuffed with delights and topped with exotic jams and creams.

They waited politely for their turn to choose.

Outside, the River of Duval Street flowed by.

THE BIKER

He stood carelessly, leaning all of his weight against the pay phone. His jacket was a leather-type, like Brando wore. He had an old biker's look about him. Rugged once, now maybe just a little seedy looking. A broad-brimmed, suede hat atop gray, long-ago-blond, shaggy hair. Goggles and bandanna looped around his neck.

There was no bike at the curb, no sign of anyone on Duval Street at that moment.

He talked furiously into the phone. A loud, serious, intense conversation.

"Goddamn it. It is important to me, if you'd only hear what I'm saying. Hello...hello!"

After listening to his distant connection for a moment, he shook his head in dismal disappointment. Disconnected and bikeless, he looked first at the phone in its cradle where he'd slowly placed it, then down at his hands, palms up. A fortuneless fortuneteller. He stared deeply, searching for an answer to whatever problem now gripped his life.

He sat down with a thump on a lidded garbage can. The air was sucked out of him for some unknown reason. He was deflated, shrunk. His troubles surrounded and cloaked his already sagging shoulders. His head was bowed down, chin to chest. Despondent, he sat like an empty bag, airless and crinkled.

Someone, something molecules away had pricked his skin and caused him pain. His eyes flickered. People walked by laughing, lovers holding hands. The scent of jasmine floated on the light breeze, the sound of palm fronds crackled electrically in the air.

Thunder rolled in off the ocean, loud, then the first bike appeared, followed by a second, and then the street was awash with wave after wave of them. Harleys mostly, dozens of them, riders in full regalia. Laughter and gasoline rumbled and tumbled behind them as they passed.

He turned and looked at them in slow motion.

Raindrops fell, and then a tear, and then another, as the River of Duval flowed by.

SPECIAL DELIVERY

[Editor's Note: A conch cruiser is a one-speed bicycle.]

Paco.

The man peddled his conch cruiser up Duval Street, wearing a starched white shirt and Windsor knotted tie atop his bronze, gaunt frame. A proud figure.

Everyone waved to him as he glided by. An old man, wrinkled by decades under the searing Key West sun. His bicycle, looking nearly as ancient as he, its balloon tires bulging, carried special cargo today.

Hunched over with his hands high on the handlebars to support his aged bones, the man's rhythm and determination carried him slowly, surely, to his destination.

Hanging precariously across the bar in front of him, within the arc of Paco's protection, sat a bundle of ragged clothing with stick legs and arms protruding.

Jaundiced eyes and a toothless smile flashed a greeting as Paco traversed the street, scattering chickens in his wake. A battered straw hat, perched on the head of the huddled bundle, tilted leeward.

The bicyclist waved familiarly to passersby, who all waved and called greetings in exchange.

"Paco, where you goin'?" asked a boy walking a dog.

"Papa's day at the clinic," Paco answered, nuzzling his cheek to his father's back. The elder man, with one arm around Paco's neck, pulled his son's head closer to his ancient lips. The parchment-thin skin above his cheeks wrinkled as he talked. Paco nodded in agreement with the whispered request, peddled to the curb and called to the boy with the dog.

"Café con leche," he said, holding out some bills and pointing in the general direction of an opened windowed shop. "Papa needs some courage before his visit to the doctor." The boy came over and exchanged the leash he held for the offered money, then scrambled to the counter to place the old man's order.

The tiny, longhaired dog sat looking after the boy, then up at Paco, then back towards the boy again. Worried. Paco spoke soft words to the small animal, who barked in anticipation.

The boy returned with a brown paper bag and handed it to Paco. In turn he retrieved his dog. The old man silently mouthed some words of thanks and slowly reached over to touch the boy's head, just once.

Paco pushed his bike away from the sidewalk, waved to the boy and, signaling his intentions to turn at the corner, continued on to deliver his valuable package.

TROUBLE IN RIVER CITY

It is mid-week and relatively quiet in Key West. Fantasy Fest and its hedonistic excesses are over until next year, and the devoted, balloon-festooned Jimmy Buffett fans, the Parrot Heads, have not yet flocked into the southernmost city.

It is 8 a.m. and Duval Street is barely awake. A lone jogger, her bronze body glistening with sweat, prances in a gazelle-like gait as she bounds gracefully along Duval Street. The noisy buzz of leaf blowers is pushing the previous night's spillage and debris into the gutters in expectation of the bristling swoosh, swoosh, swoosh of the street cleaner's mechanized monsters.

The thoroughfare is left amazingly clean. Two dogs, one a tall black bruiser, a heavyweight with white socks, and his buddy, a short, stocky Chihuahua-mix, bounce carefree, Mutt-and-Jeff like, down the middle of the street.

Opposite them, clucking his way in their direction is a shimmering, preening Key West rooster. A gleaming green and gold with a bright red crown topping his head, he looks like trouble. The street is almost empty and echoes the flutter of the rooster's flapping wings as he stops and stares at the approaching duo.

The dogs give the fowl the once-over and decide that discretion is the better part of valor. They peel off, making a hard left, just feet before reaching the rooster, who firmly stands his ground, head bobbing, eyes fierce. Even Frank Perdue would have to admit this is one tough chicken.

A man stands in front of the Banana Café on Duval Street and waves to my taxi as I pass. He looks lost rather than interested in a ride, and I pull over and ask if I can help. He tells me that he has been walking for hours and has not yet been back to his hotel to sleep. He doesn't really need a ride, he seems more interested in talking. He and his lady friend have been down in Key West for several days and had a huge fight the previous evening.

"It was a whopper," he confided, "and I think I said some things that I shouldn't have said. Now I don't know what to say."

His hotel is only a short distance away, and when I drop him off I tell him that, I too, often manage to fit my very large foot into my much smaller mouth, and remind him that "I'm sorry" is always a good start. He only nods as he walks away from my taxi. At the entrance of the hotel, a young woman is waiting. She greets the man with a hug and a smile.

Later, as the morning progresses, an old man dozes against a gumbo-limbo tree just yards off Duval Street. He is well weathered. His tattered sandals, cracked and broken, hang precariously from his swollen feet, duct tape wrapped around the torn soles. His shorts, stained and grimy, cover little of his insect-bitten legs. Hatless, the shade that the tree offers is almost insignificant.

The man is motionless other than for the rise and fall of his chest and his labored breathing. His great, gray beard, like a fleece blanket, ripples in the soft sub-tropical breeze as people step cautiously past him.

A police car passes and stops. An officer approaches the sleeping man, leans over and gently touches his shoulder. Rocked back and forth slowly, the old man wakes, and with a resigned gesture nods his head and says something to the police officer, who offers only a shrug of his shoulders.

He pats the old man on the back and walks back to his car. He looks at the man again, shakes his head and drives away. With some difficulty, the gray-bearded man rises, gathers a small bundle that was tucked in by his side, runs his fingers comb-like through his beard, and shuffles along the street, shaking sleep from his body and soul.

The man is among a growing number of indigent snowbirds, who opt to escape the harsher northern winters and trade subway grates in New York City, for a kinder, gentler existence of abandoned boats, mangroves and the streets of the southernmost city.

Standing on the corner, near where the man had been sleeping, two couples with colorful balloons atop their heads laugh at an exchanged joke. Cruse ship passengers walk by dressed in polyester shirts camouflaged with palm trees.

The Conch Tour Train, bells chiming, crawls down Duval Street past points of interest and splendid places to spend the coin of the realm.

For some, life is good, but for others, it is only a challenge.

For some, life is sweet, but for others, all that can be tasted is the bitter.

TELL ME A STORY

L ike images out of a storybook:

Once upon a time a man sat quietly sipping from a cup of pale liquid. Next to him sat a dog, and on top of the dog sat a cat, and on top of the cat sat a mouse.

In the beginning an angel stood, hands clasped in contemplation, seven feet tall with wisps of wings adding balance to a dream-like presence. She surveyed all who passed by through silent lips and smiling eyes.

There once was a young girl wrapped in scarves of color and wonder, who danced and whirled as she played a gypsy violin between the granite pillars of a great building.

A long, long time ago there lived a boy with yellow hair. He walked and walked from one end of the town to the other, reading proclamations of doom and gloom, of prophecy and fancy, of fact and of fiction. He held his book in front of him like armor to protect himself from demons that followed close behind.

In a little kingdom by the sea a woman sat leaning against the front of an aged structure. She spoke harshly to passersby who stared at her, and spoke more harshly to herself when she was alone. She was the queen of her domain and did what she pleased when she pleased. "Let them eat cake" and "off with your head," echoed behind her as she pointed and scowled her way through the day.

Once upon a midnight dreary, men rode shiny beasts that belched smoke and fire as they devoured the roadway. Black leather and polished chrome filled the silent air with acrid flavors and pounding pistons.

"Now I lay me down to sleep...," whispered the short man as he and the much taller woman pushed the three-wheeled strollers through streets wide and narrow, calling out warnings as they went. Their two huddled children slept, indifferent to the throngs of people that parted magically before them.

The children dreamed of ice cream and swimming pools, and they did not wave to the man and his dog and his cat and his mouse as they passed. They dreamed of movies and popcorn and cared not that the beautiful angel smiled at them as they passed. They slumbered, smiling as the blond-haired boy walked by, booming tales of "Animal Farm."

They were undisturbed by the ranting queen or the steel monsters that passed. They slept, still and at peace, as the River of Duval flowed on.

A TECHNICOLOR VORTEX

The doorway at Sloppy Joe's exploded in a flurry of 2 a.m. activity. The man expelled into the street staggered from storefront to curb, from curb to sign post; a pinball wizard seeking a balance that would not, could not, come.

Trying to navigate with a semblance of dignity through an alcoholic haze of undulating and swaying objects that appeared solid one moment, quicksilver the next, he swayed, tripping foot to foot.

"A dance of fools," passersby commented with both disdain & humor.

"Poor soul" or "drunken bastard" or some such obscenity followed, from those who were thankful that tonight, at least for tonight, they were better than he.

His emotions, unfelt by drug induced nirvana as the street swept by him in a slow motion ballet … pirouette…jeté, left him confused and puzzled. Not quite aware of his awkward mobility, the man moved on.

He walked tentatively to the curb and looked at the approaching traffic. Blurs of colored light flashed by his gaze in a Technicolor collage, the brightness escaping from the black envelope of night causing him to flinch and turn his head. He stepped into the flow of taxis and cars. Horns blew, and brakes screeched in anger. The booming bass of a passing vehicle reverberated through the darkness rattling teeth and windows in its wake.

A world of watercolor hues peeling from the senses of reality in soluble streaks of alcohol-tainted sensibility, strained the limits of his consciousness. He stood for a moment transfixed, gaping at the world spinning around him. Then he started to slowly whirl, then faster and faster still. He was a dervish of flailing arms. His long hair whipped behind him in a vortex of movement. His white shirt open and flapping, he started to laugh and shout like a frantic gull trapped in the intake of a jet engine.

The flashing red and blue light made its way slowly towards the man who stopped his twirling at its approach. He squinted toward the blinking lights with a question that was trying to find its way to a part of his being that was still tethered to reality.

Seeking answers but finding none he stumbled back to the curb, to find only blackness in its finality as he slammed cold and numb, face down in gutter grit, as the River of Duval Street flowed by.

The Curry Mansion Inn & Museum
511 Caroline Street

IV

Love

I am an incurable romantic and love, in any shape or form, sends me right out in search of roses, inspires me to write luscious poetry, and always brings a smile to my face. Key West, replete with a hot, steamy subtropical climate and Technicolor horizons, has become a Mecca for lovers of all persuasions. Couples stroll the streets holding hands under a canopy of picture-postcard perfection. Tall palm trees sway against the backdrop of the bluest of skies, doves coo their sweet melodies, and the mockingbirds only sing of love. The air is alive with delicious fragrance and joined hearts.
If you can't fall in love in Key West, you're just not trying!

GLADYS

G ladys was a woman on a mission. She had
arrived in Key West the day before, having
spent many hours on a Greyhound bus, and was still,
she told me, "exhausted."

She lives not far from Nashville with her boyfriend,
Teddy, who drifted into her life years back when he
showed up on her front porch and introduced himself as
a friend of her ex-husband, Conrad. He said they'd
played some blues together out West, and the banjo
hanging over his shoulder attested to that.

"He needed a place to stay for a week or two, and
Conrad had told him what a soft touch I was. My daddy
always told me to be kind to those less fortunate. I
should'a never let him in." Gladys was shaking her head
as she told me this story. "But Teddy has this little-boy
look about him, he's no more than 5'5" or 5'6", and he is
cute as a button. He has an artificial leg with a tattoo
stenciled on it, since he lost his real leg in Vietnam. I
should'a never let him in. But, I did, and we have been
together for nine years," she said.

Gladys was in Key West looking for Teddy, who
had left Nashville almost 5 weeks before. He called her,
she said, "only that one time," to tell her that he wasn't
coming back just yet, and would she please just pack up
his stuff and store it in her garage. "Told me not to get
excited, but that he had met some nice people and was

going to 'hang down here a bit.'"

"It's not that he left, it's how he left that ticked me off. Got me madder than a rattlesnake up a tree," she said. She was a soft-spoken woman, her voice warm and sweet, like summer corn. Her anger had a resigned, dignified quality to it, and she smiled all the time she was telling me her story.

Gladys is a petite woman with a giant personality, bright red hair and a whole lot of Dolly Parton in her voice. I had no choice but to like her. She looked to be in her mid-fifties, but she slyly told me that she was 70-something. "It's in my genes, I guess. My daddy was 93 years old and he still looked like a young man when he died. But he was deaf as a door."

Key West is a tiny dot of an island, two miles wide by four miles long, and sooner or later you're going to find your man, especially if you're looking for a short, one-legged guy with a tattoo on his prosthesis and a banjo strapped to his back.

It was late in the afternoon, and we were stopping at various music spots and hangouts around town. Gladys would hop out, ask a few questions, and then get back in, and we would be off to the next stop. It did not take long.

We had stopped at Higgs Beach, which is a wonderful strip of sand on the Atlantic Ocean side of the island, that is constantly bathed in soft tropical breezes, salt air, and an eclectic array of characters. Gladys came back to my taxi with success written on her wrap-around smile. "Yep, he's been here and he will be back. I'll just hang around and wait for him. Won't he be surprised?"

I was not going to hang out and see the final chapter, and so I asked, "Do you know what you're going to say to him when he shows up?"

"I do," she said emphatically, the smile still hanging there, but with a little cat-that-swallowed-the-canary twist to it now.

"I just want to look him in the eye and tell him he

can't come home no more. And that at my garage sale last week, I sold all of his stuff that he wanted me to pack and store for him. It all went cheap, too," she added with an extra dose of molasses attached to her syrupy Tennessee twang.

Gladys winked at me, and as I turned to drive away she added, "My daddy also told me not to get mad, just get even."

My guess was that Teddy was going to be strumming the blues that night.

A LOVER'S PARADISE

No matter how busy I am while driving through the streets of Key West, I always manage a smile each time I see a couple strolling and holding hands. You know, the casual stroll that lovers claim as their own.

Key West's added ingredient is that the couples come in assorted denominations: boy-girl, girl-girl, boy-boy. They all have that special look in their eyes and grace in their step that tells the tale. Love is in the air in Key West.

I recently picked up a nervous couple from Chicago. The woman, wearing a white dress and a flower wreath atop her head, had a schoolgirl's cherubic smile surrounded by cherry red cheeks. And she was beautiful. Her partner was all in white as well, except for his sneakers that were just a shade off key lime green. He carried a small bouquet of red roses bound together by white lace.

"We're getting married in about an hour," she chimed, handing me a brochure with the name of one of the sunset cruise boats on it. "Can you get us there quickly? My buddy here is getting cold feet, and I want to get this over with before he changes his mind...again."

I looked at her beau, who gave me a pretty weak smile before blushing and turning away to look out the window as we headed off to Key West Bight and the end of his bachclor days.

The woman, talking up a storm, exploded with excitement. "No one is going to believe that we did this! We came for a week and finally decided to do it, and here we are. They're going to marry us at sunset on a boat, and I can't believe it's happening."

The groom was still silent. He was so nervous you could hear his bones rattle. He hadn't said a word since getting into the cab, but finally managed a meek, "We really should call the kids and tell them about this before we do it."

Throwing caution to the wind I asked, "How many kids do you have?"

The bride bubbled back, "Four, and they will be so excited when we call."

"How old?" I trudged on.

"The oldest is 23, the youngest is 17. My sweetie here and I just never got around to making it legal. And every time in the past 25 years that the topic came up he wanted to know 'what's the rush?' Now he's popped the question and we're doin' it."

I pulled to the curb at the Key West Bight and pointed out the mast belonging to the boat they were about to board. I wished them the best of luck, and they were off. The bride's excitement had spilled over to her previously lethargic partner, who now seemed to be in the spirit of the occasion.

As they walked down the dock they held hands, swinging them back and forth to a rhythm all their own. The ebbing sunlight followed them, illuminating their way. As they reached the boat they turned and waved to me. In the distance they looked like the little figures that sit atop a wedding cake. The groom's lime green sneakers added a Key West touch to the scene. The air was warm and pungent with a special spice to tweak the senses.

In love and in Key West, it all goes hand in hand.

I think I need a hug!

How wonderful!

PERFECT PLANNING...GIVE OR TAKE AN HOUR OR THREE

How does one plan for a wedding here in Key West? The answer was a simple one for Joan from Cleveland, or so she thought. Plan it five months in advance, and nothing can go wrong. Right? Wrong!

Joan and her intended flew in on Friday, armed with the perfect itinerary: leave Cleveland early morning, fly into Miami, and catch a quick puddle-jumper to Key West. Then a speedy cab ride to The Westwinds, a lovely Old Town inn, unpack, and enjoy a casual cocktail around the pool. Then, reluctantly, Joan would leave her intended and leisurely continue on to her 3 p.m. appointment with her hairdresser, leaving her plenty of time to get back to The Westwinds. She would then dress appropriately for her 5:30 p.m. wedding, which was to take place aboard The Dream Catcher, and she and Rick would sail happily into the sunset.

This was the plan set in motion by Joan in October of 1999. Rick, bless his heart, was to be kept in the dark about all details of the event. He knew he was going to be married in Key West, but that was all he knew. (Not yet married and well trained already.) Joan had planned it meticulously.

But Murphy's Law reared its ugly head and the plan developed several rough spots, including a delay on the first leg of the journey due to bad weather, plus a mechanical delay on the second leg of the journey. The couple arrived in Key West with 15 minutes to spare. They wound up in my cab, sharing the ride with Karen and Maggie, two health care professionals from Detroit, who promptly volunteered to drop the newlyweds off first. A grateful Joan, now near tears and a nervous breakdown, couldn't believe that after five months of planning, her window of success had been narrowed to a mere 15 minutes. "He's always forgetting things, so I took over all of the arrangements. I picked St. Patrick's Day so he wouldn't have an excuse to forget our anniversary. And I've blown it."

We reassured her that all would be well. That was before the first ROAD CLOSED sign appeared, and traffic on Eaton Street began to build.

But the Taxi Gods were with us, and this tale has a happy ending. I deposited Rick at the Inn, then continued on to the hairdresser to deposit Joan at exactly the stroke of three. She insisted on paying Karen and Maggie's fare from the airport as a thank you, and with farewells and good wishes fully conveyed, I, with Karen and Maggie in tow, continued on to The Rainbow House.

We laughed at the events, and how caught up we had become in rooting for the success of Joan's St. Paddy's Day marriage. I thanked the couple for their kindness in agreeing to get Rick and Joan "to the church on time."

Karen responded, "We couldn't do anything other than that. Our first anniversary is today and it has been a pleasure to share it like this."

Nice people! It was a Key West kind of moment.

A VALENTINE'S DAY TALE

The couple wanted to go to Fort Zachary Taylor to see the sunset. Not an unusual request.

"And could you wait for us just a few minutes?" They explained that they were running late for some iced champagne, but just needed a minute at the beach.

"The last time we both saw a sunset in Key West was in 1962 when the beaches were lined with missile batteries, and we all thought that Armageddon was just 90 miles and ten minutes away from happening."

Janice and Will, who live in Michigan on the upper Peninsula, were here for a vacation and anniversary trip.

"We were married one year ago on Valentine's Day," Will told me. I must have had a somewhat confused look on my face, when Janice picked up their story.

"Will and I were both stationed here during the Cuban Missile Crisis. Neither of us was married at the time and we were...well, good friends, and we both loved to watch the sunset. It was a special time for us."

"It was several months of fear and love," added Will.

Then it was over, and Janice was shipped out to the West Coast, and Will found himself at a base in Hokkaido, Japan. It would be forty years before they saw another Key West sunset together.

They had tried writing to each other, but the letters became postcards and then, pretty much by mutual agreement, they stopped altogether.

"I never forgot Will, and whenever I looked at a dazzling sunset I would remember how we'd held hands tightly until the sun set over the ocean, and then we would hug."

A precursor to today's Sunset Celebration, I thought, only without comedians and bagpipes.

Both Will and Janice had lost their long-time spouses to cancer several years ago, and both Will and Janice had individually visited Key West in 2000, Janice with her 35 year old daughter in tow.

"I went to the beach for a touch of nostalgia and got a bit more than I bargained for."

Will was shaking his head in wonderment, as he told me that when he got to the beach he saw two women standing on the rock jetty at the mouth of Key West Harbor, their backs turned to him, and the sun silhouetting them against a golden sky.

"I knew that it was Janice the minute that I saw her there. I knew it!"

It took one year to find out that they were still in love, and then, on February 14th, 2001, they traveled again to Key West to exchange wedding vows on the same beach at sunset, beholding the same magical scene that had been in their hearts for the past 40 years.

They stood at the water's edge. They watched the sun, swollen and fat with fire paint searing brushstrokes of sunlight, bright and dripping, spill over a blue-green canvas. Holding hands, fingertips actually, the couple's eyes made fierce love, their hearts tuned to a cosmic strategy that spanned thousands of miles and four decades. In the master plan of it all, only one tick of the Universe's clock. But the patience of Venus, Aphrodite and Cupid knows not of time nor space. These Gods and Goddesses know only of love.

Wishing you a Valentine's Day, every day.

A LOVERS TOUCH

A lover's touch at midnight.
I love you whispered
Through parched lips and hot skin
Joins the musky smell of loving.
Sweet sweat and
Nipples swollen and expectant
Stirs a yearning and aching hardness.
Lustful desire follows
Familiar hills and valleys,
Hiding nothing.
Open and exposed,
Thighs burn with life's fire.
Eyes, shimmering slits
To the window of your heart,
Search for your soul,
Touches your moistness that
Glistens in candlelight.
And breathless breath
Inhales you
Deeper and deeper
As heart's desire
Enfolds me.
And time and motion
Bring me to the endless stream.
The river of life,
The stairway to ecstasy,
The pathway to Nirvana.

COME QUICKLY, I AM TASTING STARS!*

I have written about many different topics in my tenure as the *The Key West Citizen's* cabby scribe, the. unofficial title affixed to me by Key West columnist, owner of the Abaco Inn, and all around man-about-town, George Fontana. Today I write about my favorite topic: A Key West Love Story.

I had picked up a fare at The Southernmost Motel who was heading out to the airport for his flight back home to South Elgin, Illinois, a suburb of Chicago.

The usual, "Hi, how are you?" exchanged, I asked how he'd enjoyed his stay in Key West. The answers to this question usually range from "great," to "fantastic," with variables in between. I was not at all prepared for the intensity of this young man's response.

"It was the best vacation that I have ever had. My entire life has been changed by it. I will never be the same again."

He used terms like "magical," "amazing," and "the things dreams are made of." He had a smile on his face he described as "perma-grin."

Jeff's story was short but sweet. He had been friends with Alyssa for over eleven years, starting when they both lived in Maryland. As time passed Jeff moved away, but their friendship endured with many visits, letters, and phone conversations. Jeff never once let on about his true feelings of love for Alyssa, and she never suspected that their relationship was anything other than it appeared to be.

A friend of Jeff's offered the use of a house in the Keys for the Fourth of July holiday, so Jeff called Alyssa and suggested that they take advantage of the offer of some southern hospitality. They planned to spend a couple of days at the friend's house, and then the balance of the week down in Key West. It all sounded pretty good to both of them. The plan was agreed to, and now the good part unfolds.

After fireworks on the night of July 4th, they were both sitting in a quiet spot near the beach. Jeff told me that they had seen seven shooting stars that night, more than he had seen in his entire life, and he had made a wish on each star. Each wish came true. The best one was that Alyssa told him that she was in love with him, and that she had been for the past eleven years. They both had carried a torch for each other. It had dimmed but never been extinguished, for over a decade.

A dream had come true for both of them. The universe had, in its magical, mystical way, woven a path from dream to reality.

Our tropical isle is a lover's destination, and continues to spin its spells upon those with hearts open enough to listen.

When you wish upon a star in paradise your dreams just might come true.

[Dom Perignon, upon discovering champagne.]

A QUIET SIDE TRIP

Several days a week, Key West receives visits from a flotilla of cruise ships. These behemoths, easily the tallest structures in the city, unload their daily allotment of tourists, who are all in town to experience Key West, for better or worse. Duval Street, the main thoroughfare in town, is transformed in a blink from a nearly deserted sleepy avenue to a bustling, hurdy-gurdy, honky-tonk scene with more sights and sounds to tickle the senses than a county fair. It is a busy time for cab drivers when the cruise ships are in port.

A round, balding man sporting a pale, northern complexion opened the front door of my taxi, his only salutation being a question, "Cuban cigars?"

My response of, "No thank you, sir, I don't smoke," seemed to displease and confuse him somewhat, as he quickly backed out of my cab and slammed the door, muttering a fairly benign obscenity, before flittering off and blending back into the crowded street.

The next half-hour brought an assortment of people, some just asking directions to a shop or museum, which I am always pleased to share, and others actually wanting a ride to a desired location, which I am also pleased to provide.

A well-dressed couple approached my taxi in front of the Custom House Museum, a great red-brick building that dominates one end of Front Street, adjacent to where the cruise ships dock. They wanted to go to Sugarloaf Key, about 17 miles north of Key West on U.S. Route 1. Fred and Linder, husband and wife, were on a journey.

"We need to make three stops. The first for flowers, maybe yellow roses, then at the cemetery on Big Coppitt to visit my mother and father, and then on to their old house on Sugarloaf Key," Linder said.

When Linder went into the florist to find her mother's favorite flowers, Fred told me that the cruise was a birthday trip for his wife, and the little side excursion was an important part of it for her. I also learned that Fred is Judge Fred J. Berman, a circuit judge in Broward County. He is also an avid reader of mystery novels.

"I stalk the halls of justice between sessions reading detective stories," Fred confessed, and we shared some favorite authors while we waited for his wife.

Linder came back with a pretty bouquet of yellow tea roses in hand, and we headed to the cemetery on Big Coppitt Key.

The cemetery, set back at the end of a dusty road, is a serene plot of land surrounded by mangroves and the turquoise waters of the Gulf of Mexico. It is flat, as are most of the Florida Keys, and has only a thin ribbon of roadway leading down its center. Low headstones are set into the landscape to mark loved-ones' resting places.

I stopped my taxi, and the Bermans left my cab and tentatively walked across the quiet lawn, careful that their footsteps not disturb even a blade of grass. They stopped before a pair of granite markers that lay warming underneath a bright Florida sun, both perhaps unaware that around them the mourning doves cooed and mockingbirds offered an eclectic repertoire of songs. Several feet away a flock of Ibis, some young and still pink-feathered, pecked at the earth. Linder Berman, tears welling in her eyes, looked down at the place before her. The Judge moved close to his wife and placed his arm tenderly around her, her head slowly finding a place of solace upon his shoulder.

For an instant, time seemed to stop. The images before me were a still-life framed by the window of my taxi. Overhead, a wing of Navy jets flew in formation, carving out space, breaking the gentle air and shattering the spell, as serenity was replaced by reality.

The Bermans made their way back to my cab, and we completed the journey, on up to Sugarloaf Key and finally back down to Duval Street.

"Most of the people on our cruise probably spent the day parasailing or swimming. Won't we have an interesting conversation around the dinner table tonight?" observed Linder, laughing. "We went to visit mom and pop today. We brought flowers, but they didn't have much to say. And how was your day?"

I returned Fred and Linder to Key West, and we said our good-byes. It had been an interesting morning with nice people. Before the cab door had closed, a familiar face appeared at my window and asked, "Cuban cigars?"

It was the same guy as before, asking the same question. I wondered how many cabs this fellow had stopped in his quest for that elusive prize. And because all pink cab drivers must look alike to him, the redundancy in asking me that question twice would have escaped him.

Shaking my head, and singing, "No we have no Havanas," I slowly pulled out into the current of the street, the man's newest profanity lost in the pulsing rhythms and vibrations of Duval Street.

HEARTBREAK HOTEL

Well, since my baby left me,
I found a new place to dwell.
It's down at the end of lonely street
at Heartbreak Hotel.
...Hey now, if your baby leaves you
and you got a tale to tell,
Just take a walk down lonely street
to Heartbreak Hotel.
—Mae B. Axton, and Tommy Durden

Two people. A man and a woman, looking at each other and smiling a lover's knowing smile. She had just quit her job. "The boss told me to wear shorter skirts, so I told him what to do and where to do it." And he had recently been fired from his job on a fishing boat operating out of Stock Island. "It was the worst boat I've ever been on. I'm glad I got off of it alive."

The couple had gotten into my cab on Duval Street amidst a flurry of cruise ship passengers. He was unshaven and they both wore cut-off jeans trimmed short, each one showing a bit of cheek. And both had a fairly good alcohol-induced buzz going.

"We're gonna get married this afternoon and I need to find something nice to wear."

"Inexpensive," he added.

"And then a ring. A pretty one with rubies. That's

my name, Ruby. And I always did like them."

He chimed in again, "Inexpensive, O.K.?" They were holding hands, sitting real close, doing some pre-nuptial bonding.

I mentioned a couple of consignment shops that I knew of, and off we went. I waited outside of the first shop on White Street, and in a short while the couple came bounding back out to my taxi, she waving a crown and veil, and he holding a velvet ring box, and wearing a sheepish smile. "No dress yet," they said. "This is so beautiful, and the ring is amazing." She was stroking her veil with one hand and her intended's thigh with the other. More prenuptial bonding.

At consignment shop number two, she said, "Hon, you stay here. It's bad luck for the groom to see the bride dressed up before the wedding." And out she went, leaving me and her 'Hon' to chitchat. He told me that he met Ruby only a few days ago, the same day that they both had lost their jobs. They bumped into each other at a local watering hole on Elizabeth Street, and one word led to another, as conversations usually do, and before long, life histories were being exchanged along with their recent tales of unemployment woe.

He told me that he'd been married twice before, and that three was his lucky number. "Ruby's never been married, but she sure warmed up to the idea when it got brought up," he confided softly, nodding as he said it. "Three, four days you can find out as much about a woman as you're ever goin' to." 'Hon' said this definitive-ly. He had no doubts . No equivocations.

"Ruby is the one for me, period. When I asked her, she nearly knocked me off of my barstool. Funny thing, we're both from Texas, from towns not twenty five miles apart. Maybe we shopped in the same stores, bought gas at the same station. Ya just never know."

Ruby came running out of the store carrying an off-white, lace-collared dress. She would look every bit the bride-to-be. 'Hon' was impressed. So was I.

"How much?" he asked. She told him. He went ballistic. They fought, screamed, scratched, cursed, and spit. Discretion being my middle name, I excused myself and, making sure that the meter was still ticking, I stepped out of the cab and the line of fire. When the shouting ended and the cab stopped rocking I ventured, cautiously, back in.

Ruby was climbing all over her soon-to-be groom, kissing him and touching him everywhere...everywhere. I noticed that one of his eyes was starting to swell shut and that a soft purple sheen was rising just beneath it. The first round looked like it had gone to Ruby. Aaah, love, hate and alcohol; not quite the tried and true components of a successful relationship. The cab was becoming a bit steamed up, so I asked, "Where to?"

'Hon' responded, "We took a room for the week up Duval Street a way. A place called The Heartbreak Hotel."

Ruby's lips were firmly anchored to a spot on 'Hon's' neck that I thought to be uncomfortably close to his jugular.

"You know where that is?" he said, between sucking in deep gulping breaths of air. The pre-nuptial bonding was starting to look like hard work.

"That would be the 700 block of Duval," I told him. "I know exactly where it is. It's down at the end of a lonely street."

And wouldn't Elvis have loved it?

Thank ya, thank ya very much.

ELVIS ON EBAY

The middle-age couple sitting in the back of my cab had no set destination in mind. "We'd just like to drive around and see what Key West looks like," they told me.

This is one of my favorite cab driver things to do. I get to perform my tour guide routine, "...and on your left is the town's smallest house...," talk to nice people, and visit my favorite spots around the Southernmost City, as the meter goes "tick, tick, tick."

The two were honeymooners, they told me, married just the week before. They had that lover's look about them and had known each other for a lifetime, having dated in high school. They were childhood sweethearts who, as often happens, parted, then found and married other partners. Years passed and both ultimately were widowed before they found each other again.

It was storybook stuff, fuzzy and warm and chock-full of love and pathos, but with a twenty-first century twist. As they talked, their eyes smiled. They exchanged touches, intimate and gentle. They whispered secret words, laughed at each other, laughed at life. Still childhood sweethearts, I thought.

Isaac told me, "We met again because of Elvis and eBay."

As their story developed, Isaac claimed to be the most avid Elvis Presley fan this side of the Rocky

Mountains. "I have a small Elvis shrine in my basement. Photos, old show tickets, albums and clothing. I collected most of the good stuff while Elvis was still with us."

His new wife was sitting close to him, holding his hand and nodding. She told me that after her first husband died, she cleaned out the attic, and came up with a pile of "collectibles" that she figured might turn a few dollars on eBay, including a few Elvis Presley items.

"I never expected a new husband out of the deal. It's been a dream come true." She leaned her head on Isaac's shoulder, a wistful, contented smile on her lips.

People trading on eBay use code names such as Spock24 or Strangerthanu, so the first time that either of them realized who had bought, or sold, the Elvis memorabilia was when they exchanged names and shipping addresses for their transaction. Several emails and half a dozen phone calls later, she and Isaac arranged to meet for coffee and catching-up. As the crow flies, they lived only 42 miles apart. Elvis went along for the ride.

Fairy tales can come true, the couple found out, and now they were in the back of my pink taxi doing the tourist thing on their honeymoon in Key West.

Isaac and his bride were paying only marginal attention to my guided tour, the price they paid for being in love. But when we turned onto Duval Street, alive with color and music, the sights and sounds drew their attention, like flowers drew Monet. There was a kaleidoscope of interesting sights: a young woman in gypsy rags twirling about in circles while playing a violin, a dog wearing star-shaped sunglasses napping over the arm of a folding chair, a man with a mustache wearing a stunning strapless dress, and Elvis Presley, painted gold from the top of his curly head to the tips of his shoes. He was walking along the street strumming "You ain't nothin' but a hound dog..." on a shimmering gilded guitar.

Elvis is a regular on Duval Street, his costume a steady draw for people wanting to be photographed with the King.

"Stop!" This, coming from the back of my cab, came as no surprise to me. Five minutes later, we were back in my taxi with a picture of the bride and groom, arms draped around the man who had brought them together.

We continued on with my tour. Soft breezes, jasmine-scented air, streets shaded by stately royal poincianas. The trees burning with shades of red and orange vied for our attention, and waved a greeting as we passed by. Palm fronds crackled above and around us, electric with excitement. The air was thick with the flavor of beauty and the bounty of love.

Isaac gently held the photo of the Golden Elvis, for which he was already visualizing a spot on a shelf in their basement. It would sit, he told me, somewhere between the photographs of a lean, trim Elvis, fresh and youthful in his army khakis, and the puffed-up Las Vegas version that made us all shake our heads.

The words:

> *Love me tender, love me true,*
> *all my dreams fulfilled,*
> *for my darlin' I love you,*
> *and I always will*

played incessantly in my mind.
Uh-oh. I think I need a hug.

WRITERS BEWARE

She twanged her Kentucky accent like a steel guitar in heat. Picking and strumming consonants like the Pied Piper piping. Syllables strolled a casual lover's walk along her tongue only to find your ear and the pathway to your soul, to sink down deep till your insides vibrated. Words so sugary that they had to be served up quick as a wink or they would melt in her mouth. Whatever left her lips was a love song, sweet as summer corn served up hot and buttered on a silver platter.

"Good day to you, sir." She was a Gibran tome, molten enough to make de Milo's Venus a pool of gray slag, bold enough to make it stone again. She was a slight wisp of a woman, and hypnotized me the moment I first saw her. This octogenarian lady with snow-white hair had the bluest eyes and the reddest lips I could remember.

Maggie and I were old friends in a minute. She was in town for the annual Key West Literary Seminar and looking for knowledge, intellectual stimulation, and a "good-looking, gray-haired writer" to take back to her old Kentucky home.

"If I wasn't already spoken for, I could probably run away with you," I teased, or half-teased, not quite sure how much of a joke I'd made.

"That is real sweet of you to say," she drawled.

More sugar, I thought, as the spoonful slid deliciously down.

"I'll bet the men back home are all crazy about you," and I meant it.

"Matter of fact, they always have been," she confided. "I was lucky like that. I just buried husband number six a few months back. Lewis was a nice man. He would have been eighty-five this June. He had a bad fall, went into the hospital, and just never came back out."

Some condolences were in order, but the way she told it, the words playing with each other in soothing tones and slender vowels, the bad news was just more sweet music. She gave me a brief synopsis of the passing of all of her late, later, and latest husbands. Images of a Southern Belle, collecting husbands and insurance policies, coagulated like a bad novel in a recess of my brain. But she cooed and sang a siren's tune, and those thoughts fled as fleetingly as they had accumulated.

"Mah first husband Roger, though, was mah soul mate ah do believe, and ah never thought ah would find anyone to fit so well with me. He raised horses. Then Robert came along. He invented something for the automobile industry, which they just could not do without. And, ah found out that you could have more than one soul mate. After Robert was Dean, he was an actor and just swept me off mah feet. He was a soul mate as well...." I was mesmerized. "Going to be quite crowded in the hereafter when we all meet up," she chimed. Music again.

She ticked off each of her husbands' high points: "Money, very handsome, kind and gentle, great in the sack, witty, loved animals, in no specific order," she said, twinkling at me through far away eyes. "Now ah'm in Key West looking for another husband. Maybe someone a little bit different from the others, maybe a writer."

My advice to all bachelor-writers ages 65 through 105: If you hear music, and there is no one there, it is not the suggestive lullaby of the ocean calling. It is

Maggie. If you want to stay a bachelor you'd better get out of town before sunset, because if you don't, this fine Southern lady will find you and, take it from me, you will not stand a chance.

AND THEY LIVED HAPPILY EVER AFTER

T he man and woman stood in front of the white picket fence, the Heritage House Museum and Robert Frost Cottage as their backdrop. She was a picture-book-perfect bride, dressed in satin and lace and pearls. Tiny gems graced her ears, a touch of blush and ruby red lips. Just perfect. The groom wore an impish grin, a starched white shirt, and a necktie expertly knotted. He stood tall and proud, carrying his jacket neatly folded over one arm, and holding his bride-to-be on his other. The poetry of the moment did not escape me.

May, the intended, at age 76, summed it up in eight words: "We met, we danced, we fell in love." She turned to Thomas, age 80, and her sparkling eyes filled with love as she repeated, "and we fell in love." Thomas nodded and added a solitary, "Yup."

In the back seat of my taxi, the couple held hands and talked and touched on the way to Fort Zachary Taylor, where May and Thomas were to exchange their wedding vows at sunset. Between them, May told me, they had six sons and seven daughters and, as close as they could compute, somewhere between 75 and 80 grand and great-grand children. Thomas, a man of few words, again nodded in agreement.

The couple had met while living in a seniors' community in Valirico, Florida, and decided to combine a planned bus tour to Key West with their impending nuptials. We swung around to Front Street where their tour bus and approximately 32 friends and neighbors from their community waited, and we all caravaned into the State Park for the wedding ceremony.

"Are you nervous?" I asked May.

Her eyes twinkled. "Just a little," she said. "I haven't done this since 1943."

At the beach they were met by local Reverend Debra Benedict who, armed with a video camera and a tape deck playing Perry Como love songs, started along the path to the water's edge, to the sea and the beauty of the slowly setting southernmost sunset. Along the path to the beginning of May and Thomas's lives together.

"Grow old along with me
The best is yet to be...."

Robert Browning

A VISIT TO VIAGRA FALLS

"**B**een married over half a century," the woman told me after she and her husband settled into the back seat of my cab. "He's even more cantankerous now than he was back then."

She talked at a volume that ever-so-slightly vibrated my windows. "And he was pretty bad in those days." Still shouting, she added, "And, to boot, now he's almost as deaf as a stone." The gentleman sat silently next to her, smiling and bobbing his head in agreement.

"He doesn't have the foggiest idea what I'm saying," she hollered, shaking her head. "Just deaf as a stone."

I asked her why she was shouting if her husband couldn't hear her anyway. Still bellowing, she told me that if she talked in a normal tone her husband would accuse her of telling secrets, or of ridiculing him.

"So please speak up as loudly as you can or Harry will give me a hard time later." As an afterthought, she murmured, "All in all, he's a pretty nice guy. The old buzzard. Sometimes I don't hear a word from him for days at a time. But he's always smiling and nodding his head to anything I say."

The man sat there grinning and nodding. He had his hand on his wife's knee, and I detected a little twinkle in his eyes in between head bobs.

In a roaring voice, I said that after fifty years of

matrimony, there still appeared to be a spark of love between them. What was their formula for success? The woman shrugged, smiling self-consciously, and sat back, quiet at last.

Pulling up to the couple's destination, I turned to loudly announce the amount of the fare. I disturbed the twosome, locked in amorous embrace. Ruffled, the woman smoothed her dress, adjusted her cleavage and shouted her good-byes as she left the cab.

As Harry leaned in to pay me, he looked over his shoulder to see if his wife was within earshot. She was not. He smiled, winked at me and left me with this one word: "Viagra."

THEY BE COOKIN'

T he frail, elderly couple waved at my taxi from
their perch on Front Street. They were on the
steps of the impressive Custom House Museum, their silver hair framed in stark contrast to the red brick structure. He was wearing a sports jacket and a tie, she a
pastel knit suit. I assumed, correctly in this instance,
that they'd just disembarked one of the Goliath floating
inns that make port here in The Southernmost City.

The woman did most of the talking. "We've got a
few stops to make and not much time," she chimed as
soon as they settled down into the back seat of my cab.
"Think you can help us?"

Always up to the challenge, I nodded and asked
what they had in mind.

"Mrs. Thatcher, no relation to Margaret," she said.
"I need a drug store that has hearing-aid batteries. I put
my only pack down next to my plate at dinner last night
and someone at the table must have eaten them." Her
husband, the good Mr. Thatcher, giggled at her joke as
his liver spotted hand fidgeted with the knot on his necktie.

"A travel iron, aspirin, and we have to stop at
Sloppy Joe's for a tee shirt," spilled out next on her list.

Mrs. Thatcher explained that they'd love to stroll
the town, but last year for her 77th birthday she received
a Teflon hip that "makes walking as much fun as a

Wisconsin church picnic in February. And he has enough Teflon in him to fry an egg on," she added.

Mr. Thatcher chuckled again. "Some in the strangest places, too," he said.

"Next we need a good adult book store. Someone on the ship told us about one on Duval Street somewhere that has good books and movies."

Mr. Thatcher did not chuckle this time, sending me the signal that the Mrs. was not joking.

Here again was another example of finding the absurd in the mundane, which never ceases to amaze and amuse me. I had categorized this couple as being straight out of a Disney G-rated movie. She a Grandma Moses type and he Mickey Rooney's film father, Judge Hardy. Not a geriatric Ozzie and Harriet searching for *Debbie Does Dallas* instead of *The Yearling*.

"And toys also," said Mr. Thatcher, still chuckling.

I offer no details nor graphic descriptions of the list of playthings that the Thatchers asked about, but will leave it to your imagination, which I'm sure can do a better job.

As the conversation streamed on, all I thought about was that this could be my grandmother and grandfather in the back seat, clucking and hee-hawing about the quality of latex products and XXX-rated video stars and their qualifications. The vision of my grandparents, Sam and Rose, in the sack with accessories was beyond the furthest realms of my comprehension.

The last item on their shopping list was a visit to Teasers. For those of you who are non-residents, Teasers is a local club featuring nude female dancers, or so I'm told.

"I promised him an eyeful of pretty women," Mrs. Thatcher quipped as Mr. Thatcher chuckled again.

Much to their mutual disappointment, I broke the sad news that the club was not yet open today, and that their ship's departure time would preclude a visit. We did manage to complete the balance of their list, and when I left them off near their cruise ship on Front Street, both loaded down with their day's shopping spree, a fleeting thought entered my mind. With all their Teflon implants and today's purchases, they were sure to be cookin' tonight.

TO SLEEP...

O n Wednesday of this past week I met some people who all complained about the same problem: they either could not sleep, or were not sleeping well.

Early in the day I picked up a waiter en-route to work at one of our Duval Street eateries. He was crumpled up in the back of my cab searching out a comfortable spot, and could not stop yawning. He looked like he needed a pillow, badly.

"Tough night?" I asked, catching him mid-yawn.

"Sure was, and I don't know why," was his groggy response.

Minutes later I had to wake this fellow as we arrived at his destination. Yawning still, he apologized for nodding off, and told me he just could not get to sleep the last few days, spending hours tossing and turning in search of slumber. He yawned as he said good-by. I yawned as I pulled the cab away from the curb going to my next call.

About mid-day I picked-up a young couple at Mallory Square who were vacationing here from Toronto, Canada. They, too, were listless and looked like they were ready for a pillow and a good night's sleep. Two minutes into the ride the young man was asleep, and his partner smiled weekly at me between yawns, and said that they'd been in town for a couple of days, and were having a fine time, except that they couldn't sleep at night. They were exhausted, and did not know why. She thought that maybe it had something to do with "the alignment of the planets." I dropped them off at The Radisson Hotel, after waking her beau and yawning our good-byes.

My last fare that day was a local gentleman who has been my passenger many times. His name is Robert Rogel, and he always has an interesting story to share with me. He makes the same trip each day to visit his wife of fifty-two years, who is a patient at the Key West Convalescent Center. Robert is proud of the fact he's been married for the same amount of time that he's had a driver's license. "Same wife and never a traffic ticket in fifty-two years."

With a sigh and a yawn, I told Robert about my two fares today and their lack of sleep. He told me that he has the same problem many nights; tossing and turning and not having any luck getting to sleep. But he has found a way to cure it!

"When I can't sleep, I call a cab and go out to the hospital and visit my wife. I stay for five or ten minutes. Most of the time she's already sleeping but I stay for a while, just sitting with her, then go back home and go to sleep. That's all I do."

Sleep well, Robert. Fifty-two years of practice, "...to sleep, perchance to dream."

Bone Island Bob's
430 Greene Street

V

Southernmost Homeless

Here in Key West (once the richest city in Florida), there are men, women, and children who are living without a roof over their heads other than perhaps the rusted roof of an abandoned car, a canopy of mangrove trees, or the beautiful star-studded universe.

Many of the homeless individuals are treated as criminals: for panhandling, or having a beer in public. But their most serious crime is being poor.

Some homeless become stuck here by economic, health, or family circumstances. Others live here by choice, believing that being homeless in Paradise is better than being homeless anywhere else in the world.

LET ME INTRODUCE YOU

I start my driving shift at 8 a.m. and have found that early mornings on Duval Street bring out a special cast of characters. Many of these people are permanent fixtures on the main drag and can be seen almost every morning. Their presence has become a part of the atmosphere that makes Duval Street one of The Famous Streets of the World.

Their absence also causes concern. Many are street people who have no permanent roof over their heads, no safety net of family or friends to particularly care if they are safe and well. Many are nameless and want to remain that way. Some are physically not well and others are "socially impaired" in one way or another.

Yet you cannot help but miss them when you pass by their regular spot and see that their 2-foot by 3-foot piece of turf is empty or that another anonymous soul has taken their place.

I have seen many of these folks come and go. Some return each year and some seem to just evaporate. Many travel north as the summer descends for the very same reasons that their more affluent counterparts, the "snowbirds," do. They are escaping the hazy, hot, humid days of a tropical Key West for cooler climes. When the autumn returns up north, the nomadic contingents descend back to our tropical paradise to enjoy the best weather anywhere in the continental United States. The difference, of course, is that the homeless in Key West in the winter are usually just as homeless up north in the summer.

Here are a few of these people. The names I use are my own invention, but the people are real.

Barefoot Max strolls the length of Duval Street each day. He is shoeless, and for the most part oblivious to all that goes on around him. His disheveled appearance and unkempt hair and beard travel silently with him along the ribbon of Duval Street, mute companions to his solitude.

Mary is a homeless person's anomaly. She sits against the buildings along Duval Street and follows the shade. When the sun moves, Mary moves as well. She has cropped blond hair and carries on an angry conversation with an imaginary adversary. She is also the best-dressed homeless person I have ever seen, with a wardrobe that is extensive and relatively clean.

June is a Key West fixture. She used to sit under the overhang where Viva's was formerly located, on the 900 block of Duval, but I have seen her recently in a doorway on lower Duval Street. She is a large-framed black woman who sits next to a shopping cart that carries all of her possessions. Some days when the heat rises, June sits rather elegantly and fans herself to catch a breath of air. In another era she wouldn't have been out of place sipping a cool drink under a Kapok tree.

Beer Bob sits on the sidewalk diagonally across from Sloppy Joe's. He is not in good shape. The sign set before him is an honest statement by a man who has nothing and expects nothing. His sign simply reads, "Why bother to lie, I want your money for beer."

Uncle Sam walks Duval Street and checks the rubbish receptacles on each corner for food. He wears shorts that look like the American flag, and at any time of the day can be seen from the waist down dangling out of the open mouth of one of those street corner cans, with the can looking like it's doing the devouring.

The cast is many and varied and changes daily. As my cab carries me past these folks, I wonder about their families, their lives and the tales they could tell if only someone would stop and listen.

Maybe one day I will.

AND THEN HE BLINKED

L ife's blood ebbs and flows through the main island artery,

an electric, eclectic sluice named Duval Street.
a vibrant showcase of riches to rages to riches,
a dichotomy of people layer upon layer,
from the Gulf Coast to the Atlantic Coast...
worlds apart but tethered by a one-mile ribbon
of blacktop, The River of Duval.

The little man appears each day like magic. He is a familiar sight walking throughout the city carrying several black duffel bags almost as large as he is. He is dressed all in black as well. Black leather high top shoes, worn and cracked with age, a rumpled black suit and a tattered black cloth hat. The only exceptions are his white beard and long white hair that billow in the north wind as he walks along U.S. 1.

His leathery skin is as worn and weathered as his shoes. He never stops walking. He is a slow-motion pendulum, moving as the tide, from one side of the island to the other and back again. He talks to no one, blocks no one's path. He asks for no money nor food and carries no sign asking for a handout. He is a humble, quiet old man, inflicting his poverty on no one, his homelessness his own plight. His steps are painful to watch, heavy with the weight of age, and burdened with loneliness.

He seems misplaced, someone from another era, from somewhere else in time. He could be a peasant walking the streets of a little village in 19th century Italy or a fishmonger on the cobbled streets of New York's Lower East Side. He looks confused, lost in the excitement of Duval Street, music blaring from every direction. He sees bared navels, tattooed shoulders and thighs, pierced lips.

A flurry of blue and red feathers approaches, as a woman with a Macaw on her arm pushes past him, the bird squawking,"I'm off to see the wizard," in a British accent. Another woman has an albino ribbon of snake draped around her pale shoulders waiting for her picture to be taken. His weathered eyes search for a familiar face. He finds none.

Two teen-age boys on bicycles pull alongside the old man as he toils his way down the street. They shout something sharp and insulting, laughing as they circle him on their bikes, Indians surrounding the covered wagons. Head down, he ignores them and plods on. This seems to incite the young men even more. One of the bikers bumps into a heavy bag draped over the old man's back and he stumbles for a step or two, jarred, his hat askew on his head. He almost falls, but is able to keep his balance and dignity, and slowly comes to a halt, placing his bags, his life, gently down on the sidewalk as the two young knights parry and thrust, assaulting him with curses and taunts.

The man stands perfectly still, and like a statue attacked by pigeon droppings and sulfuric emissions, he does not blink.

A man and woman walk by and tell the young men to leave the old man alone. Laughing, the bikers ignore the couple and continue their taunting. Another passerby shouts at the two and gets cursed at in return. Then another person joins in and another. A car horn sounds and in a minute's time the street is a cacophony of horns and shouts as the two young men on bikes are chased off, up Duval Street.

The old man still has not moved. The street grows quiet in expectation. It appears to be moving in slow motion. Heads turn slowly, cars crawl by, the tempo of the music seems almost dirge-like.

"You okay?" asks a man wearing a tee shirt announcing, "If it ain't beer, it ain't breakfast."

The old man blinks. He leans over and picks up the black duffel bags. One over his shoulder and one tucked under each arm. Slowly, without a word, he steps back into the street, and the River of Duval flows by.

A FEW SHORT STEPS AWAY

The man and his dog sat side by side under the protective awning of a large building, the November sun barely touching them. The dog, adorned with beads left over from Fantasy Fest, and wearing sunglasses shaped like stars, laid his head contentedly on a blanket that the man had placed on the stark, concrete sidewalk.

With guitar in hand and the instrument case open in front of him, the man strummed a few notes and looked up, then down, Duval Street. The street was quiet, with few tourists and the cruise ship's cargo of sightseers not yet disembarked. The man strummed a few more notes. The dog lifted his head and looked the same way that the man had. He, too, saw no activity and laid his head back down upon his blanketed oasis.

The man leaned over and gently patted the dog's back and said something soft and soothing. The dog lay still, only his tail wagging in response to the words. The man looked again down the street, which still showed little sign of life, but he plucked a few notes anyway and rolled a chord or two, and the melody followed.

His foot moved along with the rhythm and soon the rest of his six-foot frame joined in and swayed to the beat. He started singing and his voice and his guitar played to the empty streets with no care or need for an audience. The dog's tail seemed to pick up the beat, and before long a couple stopped to listen. A little boy leaned around them and waved at the dog, whose ears perked at the attention. Before long a crowd gathered to listen to the man and his song and to smile at the dog with his star-shaped glasses.

Slowly the crowd slipped away, and the man and his dog were left alone again on the street in front of the large building, guitar case still open, a receptacle for a gratuity splayed empty, the cardboard sign announcing STARVING ARTIST...TIPS PLEASE, unheeded. The man looked at the dog and shook his head. The dog raised his head and seemed to shrug, and laid his head down again, then sighed and dreamed of better days.

Some of us stand just a few steps off Duval Street, perhaps no more than one paycheck away from a store-front refuge or a sign that says, "Buddy, can you spare a dime?" or a place in line at Higgs Beach for a free lunch or Thanksgiving Dinner.

Just a few short steps away.

A LEG TO STAND ON

Ipicked Bill up at the Veteran's Administration's Outpatient Clinic here in Key West. He was en route to the Veteran's Administration Hospital in Miami for tests to determine whether his chronically infected leg, injured in Vietnam thirty years prior, could be saved...or not.

Bill's story began with his arrest some weeks earlier on Duval Street for violation of the City's Open Container Law. That's the law that allows moderately well-dressed, and apparently well-heeled, tourists to walk the streets of Key West with plastic cups full of booze, beer or brightly colored pastel slush, purchased from our many local pubs, but which does not extend to the shabbily dressed and disenfranchised.

Bill looked a bit scruffy at the time that he was busted for carrying his liquid libation in a plain brown bag (sans advertising) and was promptly shuttled off to the Monroe County Detention Center (aka the Stock Island Hilton) and through the revolving door marked Intake for what should have been a short visit. He was processed and his personal belongings taken, which included his smokes, a lighter, a few dollars, and the medicine for his bad leg.

Then the plot thickened. Unfortunately for Bill, a red light flashed during a computer check that showed he had an outstanding warrant issued in 1995 in Miami-

Dade County, also for an alcohol related incident. Bill tried to explain that there must be a mix-up. He had served his 60 days for that episode and his debt to society had been satisfied. But he found an unsolicitous ear and was issued a final statement advising him that "the computer doesn't lie." Ultimately, Bill was advised that he could, "Tell it to the Judge."

He was handcuffed and transported to Miami for an appearance before a local magistrate on the matter of his outstanding warrant. When he asked about his medication for his leg, he was told that it, too, was being processed.

After two weeks in jail, Bill was taken before a local judge in Miami who looked at the Assistant District Attorney incredulously and asked why Bill was standing before him. It seemed that while Bill's record did show an arrest in 1995, it also showed that the 60 days had been served and a proper release executed. There was no outstanding warrant. Oops!

Down went the gavel as the judge said, "Next case," and Bill was once again processed, although this time the revolving door was pointing out. Miami-Dade returned Bill's personal belongings, including the medicine he'd been requesting since day one of his round-up. They also removed from his cash, two dollars per day for each day of his incarceration in their fine facility to help defray the cost of his lodging. (Quite a bargain at that price, I thought.)

Now Bill, with almost no money in his pocket, hitch-hiked and walked (mostly walked) the 160 miles back to Key West and managed to get himself, and his now festering leg to the VA Clinic on South Roosevelt Boulevard. The doctors there took one look at his leg and told Bill that they needed to send him up to the VA Hospital in Miami to run some tests to see if his leg can be saved or if it has to be amputated.

This is where I came in. I drove Bill the 160 miles back to Miami, and deposited him at the VA Hospital, which, incidentally, happens to be four blocks from the jail that he'd just recently been released from.

The moral of this story is this: If you are going to carry an open container in Key West, make sure the container is advertising one of our local beer gardens and, more importantly, that your hair is neatly combed. Or you, too, could have a free trip to Miami.

NOTE: Bill also told me the following: he had only recently been added to the roster of 'down-and-outs' when the events of September 11th found him unemployed after working for the same Key West firm for seven months.

He had earned a Purple Heart for wounds received in Vietnam, and has had several operations on his leg over the past thirty years due to that injury. Bill was not homeless at the time of his arrest; however, because of that arrest and subsequent incarceration, he now has no roof over his head.

He is thinking of suing Monroe and Miami-Dade Counties, and the City of Key West for his arrest, the withholding his medication, and for the computer snafu. Unfortunately, Bill may only have one leg to stand on.

WANNA SEE MY TATTOO?

Two men, Key West street people, waited by the curb as I pulled my cab up next to them on Simonton Street. The man with the grizzled Mohawk haircut was perched high atop his bicycle and deposited gobs of chewing tobacco behind himself as I approached. His associate, a small, unkempt man in a dilapidated wheelchair, sat next to him.

"Chair's broke," the seated man announced. As the man on the bike rode away, I helped the disheveled man and his chair into my taxi. He wore army fatigues that had seen better days and an old straw hat with a wide brim, almost a sombrero.

The man slurred out his dilemma: his wheelchair was in sad shape, and he explained that one wheel wobbled and the other was stuck in a sideways position that dragged along the street if he tried to move it by himself.

Its only luxury was a matted sheepskin cushion, tattered and stained with age.

"I need to go to the beach. I've got some friends there to help me," he mumbled, as he pointed in several directions, waving his hands like he was swatting at flies.

Mario, my passenger, was inebriated, alcoholically impaired, drunk, sloshed, plastered.

"I need you to be just a wee bit more specific, "I told him, as there are several beaches in Key West.

An "Okay," whispered back was the best that

Mario could offer. Then silence.

I tried again. "So, where to?" His answer, a round-about, slowly developed mixture of grunts, waves, and sign language, was arrived at in a manner somewhat akin to pulling teeth.

Being that I was the only coherent person in the cab, I finally settled upon a destination that I thought to be the correct one, and suggested Higgs Beach, which sits on the Atlantic Ocean side of the island, the quiet side.

Mario again said okay, and perked up a bit as we started on our way.

"I'm allergic to alcohol," he told me, beginning to warm to my good company.

He smiled when he told me that, and I figured that there was a punch line to follow. I played second banana and blindly asked, "No kidding? What happens when you have a drink?"

He smiled again and hit me with the following line, "Every time I take a drink, I break out in handcuffs."

Now, I actually thought that to be a pretty funny joke, especially coming from a man who could have melt-ed the intake valve on a Breathalyzer test unit. I laughed, and Mario had found a friend.

"Want to see my tattoo?" was his next question. I back-pedaled a bit. One of the last things I wanted to see was his tattoo, wherever it might be.

But he persisted and finally took off his battered old straw hat to reveal the words, "BRAIN DEAD" etched across his weathered forehead in green ink.

Almost speechless, "Cool" was about the best that I could muster. My choice of words, while limited by the sight of this advertisement, was a fairly appropriate response. I did managed to add, "And how did you come by this work of art?" My inner dialogue, though, asked, "Gee, guy, what were you thinking?"

Mario couldn't answer that.

"Dunno. I woke up one morning about thirty years

ago and felt something on my head. Went to look in the mirror and there it was. Couldn't figure it out. Couldn't read it. It was backwards, ya know?"

I was still laughing when we reached Higgs Beach. I helped Mario out of my cab and into his wheelchair and then maneuvered him and the chair up onto the beach walkway where I left him to search out his friends.

When I got back into my cab I found Mario's jacket still on the front seat, so I retrieved it and went back to find him.

Mario had managed to get his disabled wheelchair right up to the railing of Salute, a seaside restaurant, and was chatting amiably with two uncomfortable gentlemen diners.

As I approached, Mario was just peeling of his old corn-colored hat and asking, "Wanna see my tattoo?"

HOMELESS

The couple walked hand in hand, swinging their arms to the rhythm of the sea. It was a cool evening as a Northeast wind funneled its way from coast to coast up Duval Street. These two walked as lovers sometimes do, heads pressed closely together, their bodies touching, comforting each other, whispering as they walked. They carried between them a worn, rolled-up sleeping bag and several plastic bags stuffed with their possessions.

Tagging slightly behind was a small black dog with a brown eye-patch. Between his teeth, the dog carried his own leash made of rope. He held his head high, and his eyes shone brightly, proudly, as he followed the couple.

After awhile, the couple stopped in a doorway and put their belongings on the ground before them. The man leaned over and kissed the top of the woman's head, as tender a kiss ever delivered, and she put her arms around his waist and hugged him with equal tenderness. The little black dog with the brown eye-patch sat down in front of them, his leash still firmly clenched between his teeth. He looked up at the couple, moving his head in quick, expectant movements. Waiting.

They parted from their huddled comfort and scooped up the little dog and nuzzled his face to theirs. They stroked his head and tugged gently at his ears for a minute, then put him back down on the ground.

The man wore a tattered tee shirt advertising Sloppy Joe's; it was a flimsy cover for his spare frame that night. His shaggy hair tacked in the wind, sweeping back and forth across his face. She was shoeless and they were homeless.

They picked up their packages and strolled an aimless stroll. A homeless person's stroll. But their eyes belied the vision. They looked at each other, and their hearts joined. They were very much in love.

And the little black dog, with the brown eye-patch, and the leash locked securely in his teeth, followed closely behind.

MAIN STREET, PARADISE

O n the street in front of the jewelry store, where diamonds and gold glistened on display, a man wearing Stars-and-Stripes shorts leaned into the open-mouthed cover of a street-side garbage can. One leg was arched high, in a precarious sky-hook, the other leg tethered him to reality. He balanced dignity with hunger and tipped inward, further into the can.

Dignity losing, the man hung there for a moment, his legs flailing and kicking, trying to find a threshold in the thick air. A conch train came by with its hoard of cruise ship cargo snapping pictures, but no one looked at him.

The can, open wide and hungry, devoured him as he rummaged for sustenance on Duval Street.

The waving flag removed himself awkwardly with the treasure he'd worked so hard to salvage, an ice cream treat of some kind on a Styrofoam plate, dripping and dirty, plastic spoon still imbedded.

He ate it hungrily, focusing all his energy on eating it. When he finished, he wiped his beard roughly on his sleeveless arm, tossed the spoon back into the can and walked away, resigned to the street.

He was in Paradise.

Just up the street, a big old woman with skin the color of rich cocoa sat in a doorway with her shopping cart of possessions, a last will and testament to life should she die that day. She had a black plastic bag covering her shoulders, anticipating a shower's arrival. Her legs were swathed in bandages protecting some untreated affliction. Her hands trembled in her lap.

With a cup at her feet, her runny eyes speculated enough money for a meal. But she paid little attention to passersby and asked them for nothing, which is what she received.

The street moved slowly around her. Waves of people washed by her, consciously taking no notice of her existence.

The man in his patriotic shorts made his way up Duval Street and walked past the cocoa-skinned woman. He stopped and turned. He walked up to her and touched her shoulder. Her eyes met his and he spoke to her gently for a moment. Reaching into his American-flag shorts, he pulled out a handful of change and leaned down to put it into the woman's cup. Then he turned and left.

The cocoa-skinned woman smiled.

She was in Paradise.

MIRAGE

T he man stopped and looked down at the paper shopping bag full of groceries. Someone in their haste to vacation had left this bag at the curb where Fleming Street crosses The River of Duval. The man looked around, expecting someone to caution him away from the treasure trove of riches that sat, brown bagged, before him. He backed up a few steps, examining the bag and thinking it might be a trap or a trick; that if he ventured too close to it, bells and whistles would sound the alarm and a recorded announcement would blare, "Step away from the bag. This is private property. Step away from the bag."

It was early morning and the street was still quiet. No cruise ship had yet dislodged its cargo of pedestrians to clog the main artery. Duval Street moved at a slower, simpler pace. The man, a vagrant by his unkempt appearance, took more steps back and examined the grocery bag from a distance.

He asked the occasional passerby, "That yours, mister?" shaking his head when the stranger either responded with a curt, "No," or ignored his question completely and gave him a wide berth.

The bag sat lonely now. Just it and the man, standing facing each other in a concrete desert. The man reached down to touch the bag, to test its pliability lest it be a mirage. The bag passed the test.

He licked his lips in expectation. He had a lean, hungry look. Malnutrition and alcohol were at work, his clothing was dirty and slept-in, his hair stringy and matted.

He looked around once again and, seeing no one, braved the final frontier. He reached into the bag and pulled out a plastic-wrapped container of bright golden grapes. He held them up to his face and looked at them quizzically. Following the grapes were brilliant strawberries, then gloriously yellow bananas. He laid these wondrous foods next to the bag and lowered himself to sit beside the cornucopia that flowed before him.

A bag of rolls, a container of orange juice, jars of jams and jellies followed by pastries. Sliced cheeses and meats. All the man could do was sit there and shake his head in amazement as the smile on his face broadened.

In slow motion a taxi pulled to the curb and a man exited from the rear of the vehicle. Two children sat looking out the window.

"I believe that all belongs to me, sir. I loaded up this cab with five or six other bags and left that package here by mistake."

The disheveled man said nothing. He just nodded and slowly helped the man replace the fleeting godsend, the smile still on his face as the owner of the groceries said, "Thank you," carrying the package into the cab to leave.

The vagrant still said nothing. As the taxi started to pull away from the curb, one of the children started crying, then the other. The taxi stopped and for a moment the Earth stood still. Nothing moved. The wind took a deep breath and finally the taxi backed up a bit and the man got out of the cab carrying the bag of groceries.

He walked up to the disheveled, motionless man and handed him the bag of groceries, smiled and said, "Have a good day."

He turned, got back into the cab, and with two

cheering children was driven away.

The man looked at the receding vision, then back into the bag and, slowly shaking his head, said, "Damn, no cigarettes."

STRUMMING ON A THREE-STRINGED GUITAR

A vagabond, drunk apparently, sat on the steps at the corner of Duval and Front Streets. He held a guitar in his hands and awkwardly strummed sour notes on the instrument that had only three strings. A brown bottle sat precariously at his side. He was huddled over, his back arched and tenuous, waiting for a stiff wind to bowl him, or his demons, over and send them crashing to the street.

A stream of slurred lyrics frothed from his lips. "Lay, lady lay…." Dylan meets Quasimodo.

His jaundiced skin and bloodshot eyes were enough to warn the most determined of passersby, "I am hopeless!"

He was just passing the time of day, his clothing a filthy collage of dotted and spotted fabrics. Shaveless, careless but for another drink, his brain, awash with mind-altering liquefied additives…sulfates, the bottle warned. He is lucky, though, for he is not pregnant, not driving nor operating heavy equipment. He's just trying to navigate through another day.

The man stood swaying in the wind, unsure of his footing, trying to focus on the crowded street before him.

His guitar caught the top of the brown bottle that fell and rolled toward the street, splaying its amber liquid as it descended one step at a time, to stop empty at the curb. The vagabond followed, first with his eyes and then with one cautious foot after another, finally reaching down to retrieve the now empty container.

He looked around, confused, seeking solace from the people passing by. He thrust his hand forward into a Red Sea of strolling tourists who parted at his approach.

The man's appearance and condition was an instant detour sign, *No Stopping: Infestation Area... This Person is Closed to Pedestrian Traffic.*

No one stopped.

Sitting back down with his guitar, the man slowly picked at the strings and slapped some notes with his thumb and the heel of his hand. The tempo picked up a bit and through the squinting slits of the vagabond's eyes there was a glimmer, a twinkle, a recognition of sometime past. The beat moved and a tune flowed from his hands as the three-stringed guitar came to life. A man with a drum sat down and picked up the rhythm, then a bare-foot woman with a flute, then a youth with bongos joined him.

The crowd slowed. Some stopped for a moment to listen, while others lingered longer. It was a real quartet...it was real music. It was magic rolling down Duval Street.

TAKE ME HOME, PLEASE

"**C**an I drive you home, Dusty?" I asked.

Dusty, homeless by official definition, lives under one of the several bridges that span the waterways in the Southernmost City. He has called this spot his home for the past eleven years.

Dusty is a gaunt man, his skin cracked and leathery from exposure to the intense southern sun. His beard is ragged, a yellowed, gray affair that flaps in the wind when he rides his bicycle around Key West.

I had seen Dusty in front of a Key West laundromat; a small stack of clean laundry sat folded on the ground in front of him. He had leaned his bike against the brick facade of the old building and stood waiting, patiently, for a familiar face to recognize him and offer him a ride. This day, that would be me.

His right knee was swathed in a dirty bandage as he limped over to my taxi. Dusty has been a passenger in my cab a few times before, and he is usually polite and, to some degree, usually intoxicated. Today was no different.

He told me that he had pedaled over to the laundry, but that he did not think he would be able to make it back home in his present combination of conditions, which was drunk and somewhat injured.

My pink taxi has a bike carrier atop its trunk, and

I knew that I would be passing by Dusty's destination. So I strapped on his old conch cruiser, a battered bicycle with bulging balloon tires. Its rims were painted an agonizingly bright shade of pink, exceeding the tropical pizzazz of the color of my cab by a shade or two. The seat, plumped up with stuffing, was covered with a plastic bag and held tight with a well-worn bungee cord, its elastic exposed and shredding. It was a mangy-looking bike, and my guess was that Dusty kept it that way because it was too ugly to be stolen.

There were three flashlights attached to the handlebars. When I asked him why he has so many lights, Dusty explained, "It's the law," which of course, didn't quite answer the question. But Dusty talks like that, at times answering you with a distinct clarity and at other times answering you in short snippets that sometimes come close to an actual response, or are as far afield as another universe.

I got back into my cab and asked him what had happened to his knee.

"Oh, man... this car... big ugly woman... it hurts... can't ride my bike... I sure did like Delores in the fifth grade."

Choppy dialogue, yes, but Dusty had managed to connect many of the dots, and I was able to sort through most of what he told me until his story jumped to his grade school hijinks in Portland, Oregon. There the connection failed.

"Laundry day?" my next query, was answered with a cheerful, "I was born in Oregon."

Then, "Are you going straight home?" elicited, "It's a hot one, all right."

I do not believe that Dusty was being elusive, and I do sense that there may be some shred of connective tissue in the questions and answers that we share, but that day, they were faint connections, at best.

I pulled over to the side of the road just before the overpass that was Dusty's destination.

"Looks like home," I announced.

"I could go back home to Oregon," Dusty said, but solemnly added, "I suppose everyone who I know there is already dead and buried."

The sadness in his eyes was immense.

I unhooked his bike and helped him out of my taxi, along with his laundry. With intense clarity, he said, "No free rides," and held out two dimes and a nickel.

"No free rides," I agreed, as he dropped the coins into my hand.

Dusty tucked his handful of clean laundry into his bike's basket and hobbled to, and then over, the metal divider that was tethered to the bridge. In one swift movement the bicycle and Dusty disappeared over the embankment, and he was back at the only place that he could still call home.

...AND MYLES TO GO BEFORE HE SLEEPS

Sunset's grip still held most visitors hostage as they looked for a hat worthy of their dollars at Mallory Square. At dusk, the current on upper Duval Street was just a gentle tumble of people flowing from shop to shop.

A man walked a crooked line down the street. He limped, with one leg twisted and bent at an awkward angle at the knee. He was clean-shaven with a scrubbed, Presbyterian complexion, ruddy and blushed pink. His silver hair was neatly combed and his clothing was neat as well. At first glance, he was simply a man with a physical challenge that impeded his progress along the street. It was a deceiving appearance.

He held his hand out in greeting to the few people he encountered, a smile on his lips, his cherry-red, cherubic cheeks puffed and glowing.

Nodding salutations to those he passed, he offered, "Hello. How are you this evening? A pleasant day, wasn't it?"

He limped slowly to the bench on the steps of Croissants de France, where I was sipping a cup of coffee. He reached out to shake my hand. His name was Myles, he said. He was a well-spoken and well-educated man in his early sixties, quoting Dorothy Parker, Oscar Wilde, and Ernest Hemingway. He was lonely, he was drunk, and he was homeless.

I offered him coffee and something to eat and he thanked me with his story.

"I was crossing Sutton Place in New York City and when I woke up, I was in the hospital. I never knew what hit me," he explained. He continued on, holding his coffee closely, protectively, to his chest.

Bits and pieces of his history emerged as alcoholic tangents dissected his story: advertising executive, Sutton Place, Ivy League, a fondness for dry martinis. But the sadness in his eyes told the tale and a tear drew a saline path along his cheek.

You could not help but like this man. He had a child-like simplicity about him. You knew that here was someone's partner, or father, or brother, or child, delegated to the street. Circumstances or self-infliction had deposited him among us in paradise.

"The hard part is finding a place to lay down where I won't be a bother to anyone," he told me as he struggled to his feet, "So I have to keep moving until the wee hours of the morning."

Myles thanked me again for the coffee and, with a smile again etched upon his face, was off.

In my mind Robert Frost repeated over and over, "And miles to go before I sleep, and miles to go before I sleep."

FOOD FOR THE SOUL

The two men flagged my cab at the foot of the White Street Pier, where the Atlantic Ocean comes ashore. It's the week before Thanksgiving, and another cold front has swept into the Florida Keys, unusual for this time of the year.

The taller of the two is a young man wearing cowboy boots, snakeskin maybe, and a well-worn black Stetson high atop his head. His blond stringy hair is mostly tucked in, but the sides, worn long, flag in the cool November wind.

His friend is much shorter, and dressed for a New York winter in an old torn and stained parka. He wears layers of clothing beneath his coat, what looks like several consecutive shirts stuck under a sweatshirt. Beat-up, black-and-white high-top Converse basketball sneakers complete his outfit, and limping, he drags one foot as he walks.

The two men could have stepped right out of *Midnight Cowboy*, the 1969 movie classic staring Jon Voight as Joe Buck, an adventurous young man who finds his way to New York City to escape the mediocrity of his Southwestern upbringing. In search of sure fame and success, he discovers only despair and degradation, and meets his newfound street hustler friend, the crippled Ratso Rizzo, played by Dustin Hoffman, whose driving force is the need to lie down beneath a warm Florida sun.

"We have some money for the cab ride," the shorter man tells me.

"I never doubted that," I respond. But I do doubt it, my thoughts giving me away.

"In from Miami," he tells me, as he looks at his friend in the Stetson, "but via New York and Texas. Hate the cold. Hadda get outt'a there. Woulda killed me sooner or later. Freakin' cold's what it is. Hate it."

He coughs, a convincing, northern crouppy cough, rolling from up from the bottom of his lungs.

"Mind if I smoke?" he asks.

"Sorry, non-smoking cab," I shrug back at him as he stops groping for his cigarettes, and his hands dangle mid-air, with no place to go. Ultimately, he puts them in his parka pockets.

The younger man sits quietly, looking out the window, his eyes big and sad, his face a long, drawn, puppy-dog face.

"Homesick," the man in the basketball sneakers tells me. "He wants to go home for Thanksgiving and maybe see if his family would be happy to see him. We've been traveling together for two years, and holidays get him right between the eyes. I got nobody," he tells me. "I went back home once, and they were almost all dead, my family. And the ones who weren't didn't hop up and do the jig when they saw me. 'Cause I looked like a bum, I guess. Never went back."

He's shaking his head as he tells me this, and he hacks out another cough. This is reminding me more and more of *Midnight Cowboy*, and I actually look around to see if anyone is hiding behind a palm tree with a movie camera filming this scene as it unfolds.

"So, can you help us out here?" he asks.

I am not real sure about what the man wants of me, so I ask in return, "What can I do for you?"

This simple question can lead to the opening of a Pandora's Box of unusual and perhaps costly requests, but I remember a past holiday that I spent alone, apart from family and friends. I remember the desolate, lonesome, aching pain that that situation can inflict. To get through that dark period of my life, I needed something that was good for the soul. I ordered Chinese food: two egg rolls, garlic-broccoli, and vegetarian dumplings. With no judgment attached, I asked, "Want Chinese food?"

Ray, the man dressed for winter, shakes his head. "No," he answers, and gives me a tilted-head, strange look and continues, "The boy would like a shower, a place to wash his clothing, and a telephone to call home. Any ideas?"

The young man looked about as mournful as a person could, with tears brimming and a joyless expression.

Key West is not a particularly homeless-person-friendly kind of town. (Last week there was a suggestion in a local newspaper that the solution to Key West's homeless problem is as easy as "rounding them all up and dumping them into Alligator Alley.")

But there are a few limited resources available for someone in need of a hand. St. Mary's Star of The Sea is one, and Glad Tidings Tabernacle is another, and is just a short distance away.

As we stop at Glad Tidings, there are a few men waiting outside for the ministry doors to open. It's a small, white building that sits placidly next to the hustle-bustle of the island's only Dairy Queen.

"I think they might be able to help to put your friend in touch with his family," I tell Ray while pointing to the church, not the Dairy Queen. He holds out some money for the short ride.

"On the house," I say, wishing them luck. I give him my card and tell him to call me if he needs another ride. They are standing in front of the building as I drive away, and Ray's hand is resting gently on his friend's shoulder.

Several hours later I do get a call to go back to

Glad Tidings, and I see Ray and his friend, again, waving at my taxi.

"We got him a shower and a phone call," Ray tells me, pointing to his young friend, "but his family didn't want anything to do with him."

The young man sighs, a deep, husky, painful sigh. He was hurting.

"That offer still open," Ray asks me, "about the Chinese food?"

It was, and we headed off to find some. I didn't have the heart to mention that the problem with Chinese food is that an hour after you eat it, your soul starts to hurt again.

About the Author

Michael Suib, an expatriate New Yorker, is an escapee from the frozen tundra of the North who found himself, after thirty years in the insurance industry, sitting behind the wheel of a pink taxi in Key West, Florida, and writing about it.

He is a free lance writer, published poet, and the co-author of the book *Meditation Express: Stress Relief in 60 Seconds Flat*, with his wife Nancy Butler-Ross.

His column, "Taxi in Paradise," appears every Sunday in *The Miami Herald*.
Mas@earthling.net

About the Illustrator

Canadian born of Italian descent, **Joe Forte** is a writer and artist who draws in ink, and works in oils in impressionistic and abstract paintings. He is the author of three books of poetry/philosophy. His work is available in France, Holland, Praha, Italia, Canada, and the United States. When not traveling, he usually roosts in Canada or Key West.

"It is through the energy of my being, connected with the materials I use, and the energy of the subjects I draw or paint that I am allowed the images that appear on my canvas...."
Fortejoe@hotmail.com

About the Editor

Nancy L. Butler-Ross parlayed her kindergarden enjoyment of cutting and pasting into an Art History degree, which now enables her to be a freelance editor and writer. She is the co-author with her husband, Michael Suib, of *Meditation Express: Stress Relief in 60 Seconds Flat*. Together, they enjoy the warmth and sense of community in Key West. Medex101@aol.com